ATLIN'S GOLD

ATLIN'S GOLD

PETER STEELE

CAITLIN PRESS
PRINCE GEORGE, B.C.
1995

ATLIN'S GOLD
Copyright © 1995 Peter Steele

CAITLIN PRESS INC.
P.O. Box 2387, Stn. B
Prince George, B.C. V2N 2S6

Caitlin Press gratefully acknowledges the financial support of the Canada Council and the British Columbia Cultural Services Branch, Ministry of Tourism, Small Business and Culture.

Cover painting by Linda O'Neill
Author photo by Archie Knill
Maps by Irene Alexander
Cover & interior design by Carol Fairhurst
Index by Kathy Plett
Typeset in Bembo

Canadian Cataloguing in Publication Data

Steele, Peter, 1935-
  Atlin's Gold

  Includes index.
  ISBN 0-920576-47-8

  1. Steele, Peter, 1935- 2. Atlin (B.C.)--Biography.
3. Atlin (B.C.)--History. I. Title.
FC3849.A85S73 1995   971.1'8504   C95-910371-6
F1089.5.A85S73 1995

PRINTED IN CANADA

For Sarah

Acknowledgements

Lotteries Yukon - Advanced Artist Award
Atlin Historical Society
Mary Burns
Derek Cassels
Ruth Chambers
Shirley Connolly
Julie Cruickshank
Ellen Davignon
Irene Fleming
Bob Genn
Pat Halladay
Jennifer Hansen
Sue Hasell
Nigel Mathews
Peggy Milius
Ken Mitchell
Bruce & Pat Paton
Lyman Sands
Diane Smith
Nora Smith
David Young

Contents

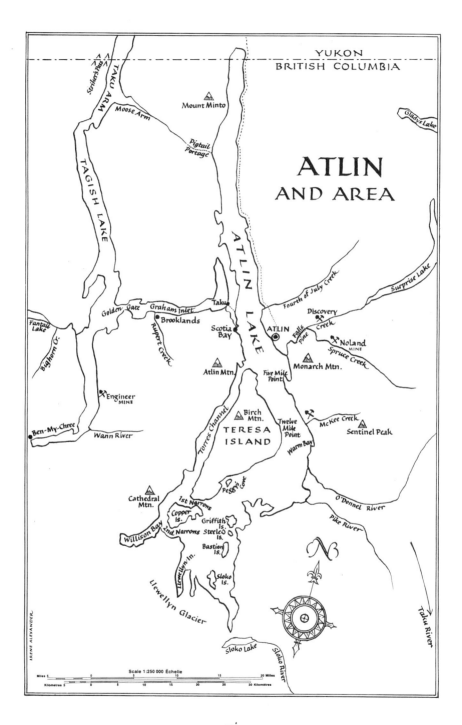

YUKON
BRITISH COLUMBIA

ATLIN
AND AREA

Scottish Pass

TAKU ARM

Moose Arm

Mount Minto

Pigtail Portage

TAGISH LAKE

ATLIN LAKE

Gladys Lake

Fourth of July Creek

Surprise Lake

Golden Gate

Graham Inlet

Takua

Discovery

Fantail Lake

Brooklands

Scotia Bay

ATLIN

Noland MINE

Rupert Creek

Bighorn Cr.

Spruce Creek

Five Mile Point

Monarch Mtn.

Atlin Mtn.

Engineer MINE

Birch Mtn.

Twelve Mile Point

McKee Creek

Sentinel Peak

TERESA ISLAND

Ben-My-Chree

Wann River

Torres Channel

Warm Bay

Peggy's Cove

O'Donnel River

Cathedral Mtn.

1st Narrows

Copper Is.

Griffith Is.

Pike River

Willison Bay

2nd Narrows

Steele Is.

Bastion Is.

Llewellyn In.

Sloko Is.

N

Taku River

Llewellyn Glacier

Sloko Lake

Sloko River

IRENE ALEXANDER

Scale 1:250 000 Échelle

Miles 5   0   5   10   15   20 Miles
Kilometres 5   0   5   10   15   20   25   30 Kilometres

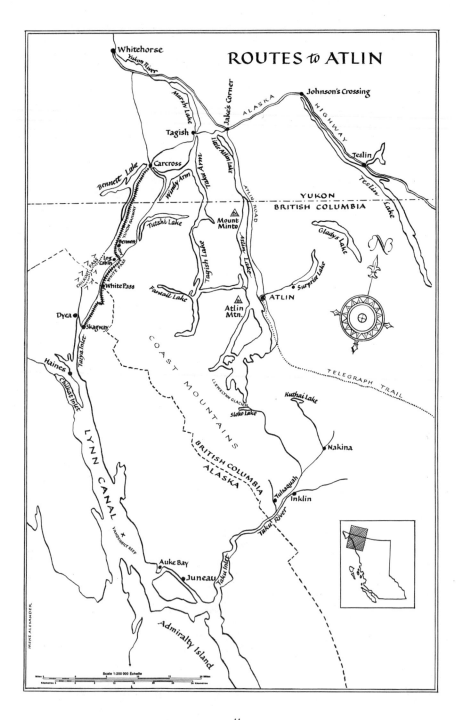

ROUTES to ATLIN

Prologue

Flying north from Vancouver to the Yukon, I am in awe of snow-clad mountains, side-lit by the westering sun. Seemingly endless peaks roll under our airplane's wings and stretch to the horizon. The land between is laid out in high relief. After two hours at 30,000 feet, and 20 minutes before reaching Whitehorse, I can pick out Atlin Lake. Many features down there are familiar to me from covering the ground on foot and by boat and small plane.

To the west, the Taku River carves a breach through the bulwark of the Coastal Mountains, and the Juneau Icecap flows into the end of the lake. Atlin, a speck in the alpine fastness, lies below. At the height of its own gold rush, Atlin was a city of 10,000 persons; now it is a mere village of 500. Straight survey lines cut ugly gashes across the forest, and the Atlin Road snakes a sinuous course beside the lake. A scar shows where miners have undermined the banks of McKee Creek with water pressure monitors and sluiced the pay dirt for placer gold. On the ground far below, people have enacted an historical drama over the past century.

Our family came to Atlin nearly 20 years ago. This book tells how we found and transformed our cabin, melded ourselves into this unique community, and absorbed its history. It is a personal story of our family's life in northern Canada — one of the world's truly wild places.

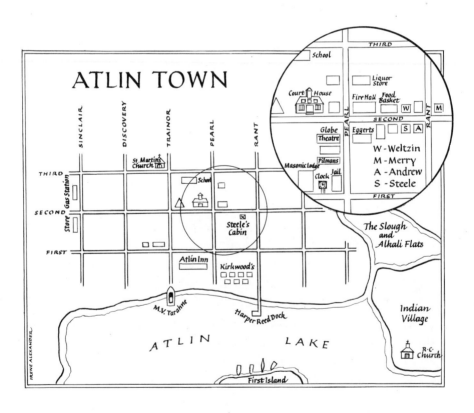

ATLIN TOWN

THIRD

School

Liquor Store

Court House

Fire Hall Food Basket

W

M

SECOND

Globe Theatre

Eggerts

S A

Pilmans

W - Weltzin
M - Merry
A - Andrew
S - Steele

Masonic Lodge

Clock Jail

FIRST

SINCLAIR DISCOVERY TRAINOR PEARL RANT

St. Martins Church

THIRD

Gas Station

School

SECOND

Store

Steele's Cabin

FIRST

Atlin Inn

Kirkwood's

The Slough and Alkali Flats

Indian Village

M.V. Tarahne

Harper Reed Dock

ATLIN LAKE

R·C· Church

First Island

IRENE ALEXANDER

The Cabin

As we drove along the Alaska Highway, heading south from our home in Whitehorse, the sun lay low over the shoulder of Mount Lorne. Back lit fox tail grass shone by the roadside where barren fireweed stalks heralded autumn. Our family was going to visit the small gold-mining town of Atlin, 180 kilometres away in the very northwest corner of British Columbia, just below the Yukon border.

Battalions of spruce and lodge pole pine stood guard on the shores of Marsh Lake and marched over the primeval limestone hills that towered above Jake's Corner. There we turned onto the Atlin Road. A yellow-gold carpet of shed leaves lay under naked aspens; cloud armadas billowed behind the volcanic cone of Mount Minto; and the mountains that flank Atlin Lake, which were so close to one another that they seemed to be talking to each other, grew ever steeper.

My wife, Sarah, and I and our family emigrated to Canada in 1975. At that time, we were living in Bristol, England. Our children were all in school, Adam, aged twelve; Judith, ten and Lucy, six. Jobs in surgery were scarce because of the post-war bulge, so we decided to leave England and the surgical rat race so that I might carve a new career in family medicine.

An aerial view of Atlin. *(Jack Boos)*

Our ancient six-cylinder Ford station wagon laboured over a small hill before Atlin. We had bought this pig of a vehicle from a fast-talking ambulance man, who had led me to believe that every true northerner needed such a monster to drive safely on gravel roads. On every outing, something or other went wrong — a broken fan belt, a blocked carburetor, or a flat tire — so we came to accept breakdowns as normal on Yukon highways.

As we crested the rise, there in front of us stood a huge chunk of mountain. It rose from a silver streak of the lake that was flanked by more mountains in a vast and empty land. Below us lay a small town, or rather a village, nestled around a bay. We drove into the town, which was like one of those cardboard models that you can cut out of breakfast cereal packages: clapboard houses with false fronts, ancient buildings that looked ready to collapse, and horses grazing on land where dwellings used to stand. We made for the lake shore, where an old boat, the M.V. Tarahne, stood on way blocks in front of the Atlin Inn. Several other boats were pulled up beside it.

The foreshore was feathered with small docks and 400 metres distant was a small forested island with some white boats moored in its lee. Further out were two more islands, one large and one small. We walked to the end of the dock and looked towards Atlin Mountain. It seemed to rise out of the lake in tiers and ribs as high as Ben Nevis, the tallest mountain in Scotland — a yardstick with which I was familiar. The southern shoulder of the mountain dipped down to a gap before rising to another equally high, but more softly contoured, mountain. Patches of snow, which remained in north-facing gullies, gave relief and scale to the peaks.

Gentle and graceful, rugged and handsome, wild and empty, this was some of the most spectacular scenery I had ever seen — and I had experienced quite a chunk of the world. In the village itself, it was as if we had stepped back a century to a world that focused on gold and all that goes with the finding of it. Even the people seemed to have emerged from a different age. They ambled through town without hurry and stopped to greet one another and exchange gossip on their way to the store. Small float planes took off from the water in front of us; boats puttered around the harbour; and a helicopter, carrying oil drums slung in a net, droned overhead. It was the Toy Town of my childhood.

The only other place of similar scale that had made so deep an impression on me was the west coast of the Scottish Highlands. Although the shapes of the hills had something in common, this was far more remote — a true wilderness. It thrilled us when we arrived nearly two decades ago, and the wonder of it has not palled in the intervening years.

The aim of our journey to Atlin was to visit Wayne and Cindy Merry, who we had been introduced to by some friends in Whitehorse. Wayne was a mountaineer of legendary renown. Their house, painted gray with white trim, had a red tiled roof. It stood

The cabin during renovation.

at the corner of Rant Avenue and Second Street on the southern side of town near the Alkali Flats. Atlin's six streets intersect at right angles with eight avenues, and on a clear, cold night you can almost hear a shout from one side of the town to the other. The Merry house's ample bay window and open porch looked across to a couple of small cabins that were tucked under a stand of willows and partly obscured the lake. A pole-fenced garden kept free-ranging horses from browsing on the prolific vegetable garden.

After tea, Judith, Lucy, and I went for a walk, while Sarah stayed to talk with Cindy Merry and Adam played with the Merry boys. A hundred metres away, we passed a small house with dull yellow and pale green paint peeling from its shiplap walls. I gave it a cursory glance and was about to walk on when the girls drew my attention to a cardboard sign on which the words "For Sale" were written in heavy lead pencil.

The cabin stood in the middle of town two blocks from the lake. An entire block of rough open space lay behind a weathered pine shed at the bottom of the garden.

"Neat, eh Dad?" said Judith in an offhanded throw-away manner. "How about we buy it?"

"Yes, Jo, it's nice," I replied guardedly. "The trouble is, owning a cabin might tie us down. And there's so much country in the Yukon still to explore."

We walked to the corner of the fire hall across the street to inspect the bright red fire pumps set on wooden blocks under an open shelter. These hand-cranked machines once fought some of Atlin's disastrous early fires. I turned to look again at the yellow cabin with the "For Sale" sign. It was flanked by rundown, higgledy-piggledy shacks of similar vintage. The cabin had a friendly face; paned windows peered across the street, and the door between them had a small peaked porch that jutted like a nose from the low-pitched roof. Pine trim surrounded the windows and framed the eaves and corners.

A porch was tacked onto the side of the house, and a small square window at the back looked out on the lake. The house faced the street away from the lake and the mountains — very much like Welsh stone farmhouses that look away from wide open valleys (the view is unimportant to farmers and shepherds who spend their days out on the hills in wet and wind).

We fetched Sarah, who, unknown to us, had already nosed around the cabin. Knowing me to be a reluctant shopper, she said nothing. We learned, at the grocery store across the street, that the house was being sold by Mrs. Margaret Veerman, who lived in Whitehorse. The store owner had the key and showed us around.

Grubby net curtains and cobwebs obscured the parlour window. A rusty pair of instep crampons lay on the sill, and flowered wallpaper peeled off plasterboard walls. An old chair stood on coffee-brown linoleum, pock-marked with cigarette burns as if a legion of black beetles were crawling across the floor. A narrow room to the right was just big enough for a single bed. A door led from the parlour into a kitchen at the back, where a small window gave a glimpse of the lake and Atlin Mountain. In one corner stood a bathtub with cast-iron ornamental feet and knobby brass taps and fittings, but there was no water tank to feed it. Nearby, on a sink that was encrusted with grime, lay a cracked mirror, some rusty razor blades, and a balding shaving brush. A lopsided stairway led to a low basement that housed a forty-gallon barrel furnace. It pushed hot air through fat aluminum ducts set in the floor of the rooms above, where chains and pulleys controlled the vents.

Sarah and I returned to the Merry's house. We held an impromptu family conference, reached an unanimous decision, and telephoned Whitehorse to offer the asking price. Within a week the cabin was ours. Therein was born a love for Atlin and our cabin that has strengthened over the years — a refuge for the family from the outside world.

Up to that point, Sarah's and my life together had been quite peripatetic. On our honeymoon, we had driven overland to Nepal and had worked in a hospital in Katmandu — she nursing and me interning. Then, we joined the Grenfell flying doctor service in Labrador, where we travelled to isolated communities along the coast by plane, snowshoe, dog sled, and boat. Back in Bristol, I was just settling into a respectable surgical job when we were invited to Bhutan by the King. With Adam and Judith, then both under the age of four, we spent six months traversing the eastern end of the Himalayas; we were among the first Europeans to do so. In 1971, I was doctor to the International Mount Everest Expedition, which collapsed just short of the summit in discord and near disaster — a long story in itself. Now, after emigrating to Canada, Sarah and I were ready to put down some roots.

Our small cabin was built, in 1929, by Jimmy Kershaw, then owner of the hardware store on the corner of Pearl and First. It stands on a nine-metre-wide by 30-metre-long "tent lot." These lots were allocated during the gold rush, when Atlin was mostly a city of tents.

Ira Bennett lived in the cabin immediately before us and, although we never knew him, he had firmly imprinted his personality on the house. At age 16, he left home in Saskatchewan and headed west with a suit of clothes, a raincoat, and ten cents in his pocket. In 1955, he arrived in Atlin looking for enough gold showing to make a living, and he spent three years mining hard rock underground at Noland Mine. The mine soon shut down because they ran into a major rock seam and had problems with ventilation. Ira claimed that the geology he needed for prospecting was learned with "two damn good ears for listening to old-timers, two good eyes, and by never using the three words a Northerner must never say: I don't know." His favorite saying was "gold makes strange bedfellows" (by which he meant that in the mining business you are likely to end up with some pretty rum friends).

When driving his dog sled out on the trail while prospecting one winter, Ira froze his feet and lost several toes. This made him walk with a rolling nautical gait. In retirement, he became caretaker of Noland Mine. We have a photo of him, with his faithful old dog Tagish, that was taken just before he died. When we first took over the cabin, Tagish, an off-white malamute husky with a lolling tongue and a rheumatic limp, came to visit and nuzzled Judith and Lucy as if to ask when his master was coming back. Some inquisitive little girls from the village made him do the tricks Ira taught him: to sit on his haunches, beg for food, and jump over a broomstick.

In front of the house, facing the street, wild rose bushes grew as high as a child's head and a boardwalk five paces long led to the front door. Left, beyond a fence of rough lumber slabs, stood a ramshackle, rustic cabin. On the other side was a small frame house, its once-yellow paint faded and peeled to bare wood. Moose antlers were stored on the shed roof.

Our lot extended beyond the outhouse, or biffy. There, piles of lumber, weathered grey with age and covered with lichen, lay among a wild garden of roses and fireweed. Intent on refinishing the interior of the house, I bought bags of nails and a book on woodworking from the hardware store. The timber was so seasoned that it was hard to saw or nail. I knocked together a sturdy work-bench and nailed it against the open studs of the basement. Each of my tools, which I hung from nails on the white-painted wall, was outlined in black to show where it belonged.

The best view was from the back of the house. Over the roofs of some cottages was the lake and Atlin Mountain. The latter, tri-ple-peaked, with snow gullies, ridges, and faces, rose 1,500 metres to the summit. The southern shoulder dropped towards Torres Channel, a narrow passage that separates the mountainous mass of Teresa (or Goat) Island from the mainland to create the world's highest freshwater island. To our right was Pearl Avenue, with some of Atlin's oldest buildings: the Globe Theatre, Kershaw's Hardware Store, and Eggert's Jewellers.

To make the most of this panorama, the interior of the cabin needed to be reversed so that the sitting room would look out over the lake. We hired Steve Baba, a carpenter friend from Whitehorse, to install a picture window. He lived alone in a shack on the bank of the Yukon River opposite Whiskey Flats. A Japanese-Canadian, short and hunchbacked with a leathery face, he had one fingernail blackened to a crescent moon by the thwack of a hammer.

"Gee, now I got this sore elbow," he said in his squeaky voice that sometimes jumped an octave. "It always happens when I start hammering."

"That's not too good for a carpenter," I said.

"You're dead right," replied Steve. "I'll have to give it up one of these days."

"What would you do if you weren't a carpenter?" I asked.

"I'd run a casino," he said. "I've always been a gambler. Specially since I gave up drinking. That's where I get my kicks nowadays."

Unfortunately the authorities didn't see Steve's idea as being quite so innocuous as he did. He did open a casino, but it kept being raided and closed down by the police, so he eventually abandoned his dream.

Steve drove down to Atlin with a big glass window in the back of his pickup.

"I think it'll fit here," he said as he eyeballed the space. "Hand me the chain saw, and I'll cut a hole in the wall." We lifted the window into place, but somehow it didn't look quite right.

"I hate to tell you, Steve," I said, "but I think it's in upside down."

"Goddamn it, so it is," he cursed.

I built a frame for the window from weathered pieces of two-by-four. The lichen that covered the deeply runnelled grain was mostly green and grey interspersed with orange and yellow buttons; some was like black seaweed. Sarah occasionally sprays the lichens with water to keep it flourishing.

Because many northern homes burn to the ground when poor quality stovepipes come apart or overheat, we got Steve to replace the old pipe with best quality, double-skinned aluminum chimney lagged with asbestos. He made a side junction to the cooking wood stove that was lent to us by our friend John Harvey, who had kept it in his garage for ages among his mining junk. The stove top had six hot plates, a small firebox, a water heater, and an enamelled back. The oven door was inscribed with the brand name Jubilee — a product of the Guelph Stove Company.

After Steve had installed the window and the new chimney, we turned our attention to the roof, which leaked. Asking around, I learned that the man for roofing was Rick Stephens, a competent jack-of-all-trades. He also helped us build a deck around the back of the house, so we could sit and look out over the biffy roof to the lake and mountains.

The timber slabs of the fence between our next door neighbour's yard and ours were weathered grey with age, and the leaning uprights were propped up with two-by-fours. Peeling bark
tinged with orange lichen exposed wiggly worm burrows. Beside
the fence lay a Chinese sluice box, its runnel drilled with holes like
a sieve. It had last been used on Ruby Creek in the thirties. Blue
Jacob's ladder grew through the riffle holes where nuggets once
dropped. Tousle-headed, gone-to-seed rhubarb peered from our
neighbour's side of the fence.

I sat on the deck and looked at mid-summer wildflowers that
almost engulfed the biffy shed in a wilderness of weeds. My old
Aunt Lilian had once told me that weeds were "flowers in the
wrong places." Rose bushes surrounded the woodpile and grew
unimpeded down the hill towards an open meadow where outfitter's horses ranged free. The horses ambled around town, from one
grazing patch to another, oblivious of traffic. For a couple of weeks
at the end of June, wild rose and fireweed flower together. Wild rose
petals, rich damask in bud, are pale pink in flower. Fireweed buds
appear first at the base of the stem, but as summer advances the tall
lances of magenta flowers unfold to the very tip, dying and falling
as they go. This harbinger of fall reminds us that hilltops will soon
be dusted with snow.

A slate grey-blue delphinium stood at the corner of the biffy
shed, and wild raspberry bushes crowded the door. Dandelion puff-
heads seeded the air and scintillated like dust particles in a sunbeam
across a darkened room. Blue chiming bells pushed up through sawdust under the sawhorse. The sun shone through foxtail grass that
waved like a field of wheat with a breeze blowing over it.

I could have spent all day admiring the flowers, but work called.
And no work was more important than improving the biffy. The
biffy stands down the slope from the cabin in a sturdy pine-board
shed, weathered by south winds that blow off the Juneau Icecap and
sally up Atlin Lake. After being exposed to the elements for many

years, the rich brown timber has taken on a variegated texture streaked with grey, black, and silver stains together with subtle tones of orange and green lichen. Rubbing a hand across the rough planks, you can feel the sharp ridges of eroded grain.

On open ground below the outhouse, horses graze or roll in the grass on sunny days and children build forts in the copse of alder and willow. There is a shortcut to the grocery store leading from the south end of town and the Indian village. An old crank engine casing shows through grass and dead fireweed, and oil stains an overgrown concrete pad of what was once a gas pump.

The biffy faces the house in full view of the living room, which discourages visitors from unduly prolonging their business. Icy breezes that swirl through cracks in the wallboards keep winter visits short. In winter, a crown of snow lies on the shed roof, and on the ground footprints tell where a visitor is bound.

The outhouse shed is also for storing stuff that might come in useful one day. Despite many trips to the garbage dump, it still contains a mass of precious and sentimental junk. A horse's harness hangs from a nail and a tattered ironing board is stored under the rafters along with skis and snowshoes. Behind the door is a large wooden box that contains hundreds of bent and rusty nails pulled by Ira Bennett to save a few cents at the hardware store. The biffy is in a separate compartment that occupies one corner of the shed. The door has a rough-hewn wooden latch on the outside, but no inside lock. Half the floor space is taken by the thunder box. A collar of polystyrene glued to a wooden seat is instantly warm to the bum — even at 40 below zero. Written on it — command or statement — is "Gentlemen lift the seat."

A short piece of broom handle set into the wall prevents the paper roll from falling down the hole. In summer, rough stirring with a two-by-four rakes the pile into corners of the pit; in winter a hearty swipe and a powerful lever action demolishes the frozen stalagmite. To clean the timber, we stand it in a metal bucket that holds ash from the furnace. Ash scattered into the hole keeps the biffy odourless without the need for lime or chemicals that stop bacteria from decomposing the pile. We avoid putting down dried leaves or sawdust which diminish smells but quickly fill the pit.

In winter, we keep a honey bucket in the frosty-windowed porch to use for a pee in the Arctic night. It is most undesirable the next morning to sit on droplets of ice left by the blind aim of a previous nocturnal visitor. The contents of the bucket freeze by morning into a yellow sedimented disc, easily discarded. I prefer to sneak down the path with the bucket in the morning rather than brave the cold midnight air.

The biffy pit was nearly full from long use. I didn't fancy digging it out, so I dismantled the old box, filled the hole with earth, and sealed it with lumber. Then I framed a room in the right hand corner of the shed, cut a hole in the floorboards, and started to dig another pit. Rather than use the shed door for access, I removed the outside wall boards. I replaced rotting studs with new timbers by raising the corner of the shed with a hydraulic jack.

I dug the hole with a long-handled, heart-shaped shovel and heaved the excavated soil into the bushes behind the shed. This monster hole was intended to last at least five years. With two other corners of the shed to use, it would be fifteen years before the entire structure would have to be moved. As the pit deepened, my respect for underground miners grew.

After digging for a weekend, the hole was gourd-shaped: wider at the bottom than the top. Soon the shovel didn't fit, so I used a short-handled spade, and Sarah dispersed discarded soil that kept rolling back into the hole. A metre down, I hit rock and needed a sledgehammer and crowbar to break it. I had blisters and a sore back, so the next weekend we hired Kendall Merry, Wayne's younger son, to dig. We lowered a bucket tied on a rope to him and then hauled out the dirt. When his head disappeared below the rim and he needed a ladder to climb out, we called a halt to digging.

I built a new thunder box and nailed a large piece of scrap copper against its inside front wall to prevent splashing. Then, I cut a hole, smoothed the edges, and replaced the polystyrene seat. Sarah's father, Max Fleming, made a weather vane from copper piping and tin in the form of a sailboat with its pennant streaming. He nailed it on top of the sloping tar-paper roof of the shed, but it got carried away in one vicious storm. He also chained a plastic-bound copy of Lem Putt's book *The Specialist*, a classic of outhouse literature, to the doorpost. It fared better than the weather vane and still entertains visitors.

After the professionals had finished the structural changes to the cabin, I set about re-fashioning the interior. Most urgent was a workable kitchen with sink, sideboard, table, and benches. Some heavy pieces of two-by-eight planking piled in the yard were overgrown with the skeletons of last year's fireweed. The texture of the deeply gouged grain felt pleasant, so I left the boards unplaned. I built a countertop in front of the window facing the porch and placed the sink against the outside wall, through which the waste pipe could drain. The cabin has never had running water, although the sink has stainless steel taps and a spout.

The kitchen, the focal room of the cabin, gradually became usable. We sat on a bench, in the corner under the front and side windows, at a solid table made of fir planks set on legs of squared logs. A sturdy free-standing bench of gnarled planks stood opposite. I had learned some rudimentary carpentry years before while building a three-storey tree house that was molded into the branching trunk of a huge oak on my brother's farm in Sussex. In the cabin, I had a similar challenge of creating livable space.

An English student passing through the Yukon washed up on our doorstep just as I was tiring of heavy labour. Stuart was happy to work for his keep in Atlin for a few weeks. He dug a ditch to lead the sink waste pipe down the hill beside the biffy to discharge into a metal drum filled with stones. The waste water then seeped into the ground through holes punched in the drum.

Next we insulated the ceiling by placing battens of fibreglass between the attic rafters. We cut triangular holes in the end walls for ventilation grilles. These would allow air to circulate under the roof and prevent condensation. Nails securing the exterior clapboard protruded into the space between the supporting studs, so we couldn't slide insulation battens into the walls. When the cabin was first built, the space was filled with sawdust and wood shavings. It made a good air trap but, over time, the sawdust had sunk, and now it filled only the bottom half of the walls. In winter, the walls felt icy cold because frost formed in the airy space above.

Stuart removed the thin wallboard that covered the spruce tongue-and-groove in each room, pried loose the top panels close to the ceiling, and poured insulation chips into the space. Then he replaced the boards.

We had to get our drinking water delivered into a barrel beside the sink. Water delivery has been a feature of Atlin life since the early days, when the town was mostly tents. One of the first water delivery men was Christopher William Andrew Neville, formerly a major in the Lincolnshire Yeomanry. He ran the Atlin Canine Waterworks and charged five cents for each bucket of water. The water was drawn from a keg that was carried on a cart pulled by dogs. Sometimes he used his horse Reno to haul a dray that had a square log water box mounted atop.

The major was a remittance man (someone living abroad on money sent from home). Usually remittance men were the younger sons of wealthy landowners whose family estates were inherited and managed by the eldest son. In primogeniture, the redundant younger males were either recruited into the clergy or the army, or were packed off to colonial outposts of the British Empire, especially Canada and Australia. The major's older brother remitted a regular monthly cheque from the old country on condition that Neville stay away and forfeit any inheritance. Remittance men usually came from the top drawer of a "silver spoon" aristocracy or from the upper classes. The rigours and discipline of exclusive British private boarding schools (known euphemistically as public schools) prepared them to be leaders in their far-flung adopted homes.

Talking of remittance men, Sarah's great-uncle Theodore served in the Yukon at the turn of the century — a strange coincidence of family ties. She owns a book entitled *The Totems of Alaska* that has the following inscription:

Presented to Constable T. V. Fleming, North West Mounted Police on his 21st birthday by Corpl. the Hon. C. Douglas-Fox NWMP Whitehorse, Yukon 1903.

Uncle Theodore was an adventurer who drifted out to South Africa to fight in the Boer War and then came to northern Canada with the North West Mounted Police. He served in Dawson City and patrolled by dog sled all over the Klondike.

Major Neville was variously described by Atlinites as "a reprobate fox-hunting aristocrat," "a real nice army guy," and "an honest and straightforward high-class Englishman." When running low on funds towards the end of the month, his water delivery service would improve and his visiting became more assiduous in the hope of being invited to tea or, preferably, to a meal.

The major came through the door of one house after packing water up a flight of thirty steps just as Winifred James, aged four, was swinging a broom, the handle of which hit him on the nose. But he took the blow with good grace. Another time, Win and some schoolmates took his horse from the barn and put it into the school basement. When the town policeman and the major arrived to look for the horse, which he treated like gold, the children, terrified they would be caught red-handed, hid under a warehouse. They managed to get the horse back where it belonged without being seen.

Later on, Walter Rasmussen took over water delivery with a horse and wagon. He collected water from the point near the Indian Village, as far away as possible from the Red Cliffs to the north of town where Louis Schulz used to dump the town garbage on the ice. It would drop to the bottom of the lake at spring breakup.

By the time Ron Bowden had become the water man, an intake pipe was laid far out into the bay. When we needed a fill-up, we hung a "Water please, Ron" sign beside the front door. The other side of the sign read "Busy at work. Enter at risk no one will speak to you." This blunt statement was often necessary if we wanted to get a job done, because, being in the centre of town, we were a captive audience to people who dropped by for a chat.

Ron filled his tanker with crystal-clear water drawn from the lake. He would park his truck outside the cabin, unwind a long hose from the side, and drag the hose between the rose bushes, through the front door, and across the kitchen to the barrel beside the sink. We always invited him to stop for tea. Ron was engaging, laconic, and humorous. As he sipped at his mug while sitting on the bench under the window, his lower jaw protruded, he grinned quizzically, and he fixed us with his louche eye. He would laugh at his own stories, squeezing both his eyes half shut and accentuating the lines of his wrinkly face.

Ron eventually gave up delivering water and now cuts firewood instead. We order a load of mixed fire kill and fresh-cut wood from him every so often and let it dry out for at least a year. A couple of cords do us for the winter — a cord being a stack measuring four by four by eight feet. We load heavy logs three times as thick as your arm through the square door of the furnace. When the grill vent on the front is slid wide open the furnace roars like a steam engine; the hot fire acts to prevent creosote from collecting on the inside of the stovepipe. We also order half a cord of small-cut aspen and willow to split and burn in the firebox of the wood stove.

The wood ritual of piling, splitting, and carrying can occupy much of a day and is an integral part of our life in the North.

Neighbours

We pinned a topographical map of the Atlin region on the living room wall to help us better understand the local geography. Taking a break from carpentry, I studied the contours of the land. Left from the big picture window — our million-dollar view — evening shadows cast strong relief on Birch Mountain's snowy, scimitar-shaped north-facing ridge. Ahead stood the mass of Atlin Mountain. Half right, one shoulder of Atlin Mountain sloped down to a flat neck of land, interrupted by the bump of Harper's Hill. Offshore across the lake, several small islands hid Scotia Bay and the mouth of the Atlinto River — a key to the region. Table Mountain rose on the north side of Graham Inlet.

In the far distance to the south just beyond the foot of the lake lies the height of land where water from Sloko Lake flows into the Taku River and the Pacific Ocean near Juneau, Alaska, a mere hundred kilometres away. Atlin Lake is drained by the Atlinto River into the lakes that create the Yukon River. The Yukon River heads north to Dawson City, passes through Alaska, and after 3,080 kilometres discharges into the Bering Sea.

The wind was rising, so I went out onto the new deck at the back of the cabin to watch whitecaps roll down the lake. A leprechaun-like figure appeared behind the slab fence that separates us and the neighbouring house.

"I'm Gerry Andrews," he said. "Drove in yesterday. It's taken me three days from Victoria." He waved at a ramshackle cabin behind him. "Come over for some tea when you've got a moment."

The previous evening, we had noticed a battered camper van drive into the grass yard next door. In the morning the shutters came off the jumble of shacks that made up Gerry's cabin. The main core of the house was about the same vintage as our own. Tacked on to the end closest to us was a shed with a steep-pitched roof. Another room stood at right angles behind the cabin.

Sarah and I ducked through a hole in the sagging fence, climbed some rickety steps, and knocked on the door of the porch, the windows of which were covered with chicken wire to protect the glass from birds and stones.

"Come in," boomed Gerry. He was then in his mid-seventies, just over five feet tall, and stooped. Wild white hair flowed back from a corrugated forehead that thrust forwards. His beard, in need of a trim, thinned out over prominent cheekbones. His eyes sparkled as he talked, and he would squeeze them closed in mirth. He wore a shabby khaki bush jacket, scuffed pants, and a pair of gussetted leather slippers.

"I'll boil water for tea," he said as he led us into the main room. "Take a seat. And please call me Gerry."

He disappeared into the porch and lit an old Coleman white-gas stove. We sat at a wobbly paint-chipped table and took stock of the room. In a dark corner beside the window facing the lake sat an iron barrack-room bedstead. A fluorescent light bulb above it was shaded with aluminum foil. A tall open cupboard held an old Huntley & Palmer's biscuit tin labelled "Sewing etc.," an Oxford dictionary, and a pile of old magazines. Gerry returned with a tea-pot swathed in a crocheted cozy.

"This is my bachelor pad," he said. "I get up here once a year alone because Mrs. Andrews doesn't really like roughing it. How do you take your tea?" He poured the tea into mugs and reached for a scarlet sock wrapped over a bottle of overproof rum.

Gerry Andrews outside his cabin, which originally belonged to Harper Reed.

"May I add a little medicine to it?" he asked mischievously. "I don't take it like that in Victoria."

He poured a liberal measure of rum into each cup, replaced the sock, and returned the bottle to the table beside his bed. He sat down on a high bent wood chair, the legs of which had been lengthened so he could admire the view over the windowsill.

"I pull that over my eyes in summer," he said, pointing to a grey sock with a piece of elastic tied to each end that hung from a nail beside the bed. "I can't sleep when it's still light at midnight."

We sipped his medicinal tea, as unlike our usual Darjeeling as Tibetan tea made from scrapings of tea bricks, rancid butter, and salt. Gerry pulled a stubby pipe from his pocket, reamed out the encrusted carbon with a penknife, and knocked the ash into a tin spittoon handy to his chair. He packed his pipe with tobacco and tamped it with his finger. His delicate hands were those of a scholar. Using a gas lighter, he set aflame a small triangle of paper grasped in a pair of stamp collector's tweezers.

"It makes a bigger flame than a match," he said as he puffed with loud clucking noises that recalled to mind my grandfather lighting his pipe. "It saves lighter fuel. This way the 'baccy burns well."

As the smoke enveloped him, he looked like Jove appearing out of heavenly clouds. From a small bottle stored on the window shelf, he squeezed a drop of bleach into the paper-lined spittoon "to keep it fresh."

We watched this ritual and listened to Gerry Andrews tell us stories of his action-packed life. He was formerly Surveyor-General of British Columbia and one of Canada's most distinguished geographers. He pioneered aerial photogrammetry, the technology of mapping, using measurements taken from air photos based on perspective geometry.

During World War II he headed a secret group of surveyors and cartographers who, in anticipation of the D-Day landings, developed a technique of drawing profiles of the Normandy beaches. They used timed air photos of waves breaking on the shore. From the separation of wave crests they calculated depth soundings to determine how close landing craft could approach a beach before grounding and how far and how deep the troops would have to wade in the sea.

Gerry and his crew surveyed the beaches chosen for the invasion landings at Arromanches. They were among a mere handful of people privy to such top-secret information. In recognition of his brilliant work, he was promoted to lieutenant-colonel and made a Member of the British Empire.

We visited Gerry Andrews again for medicinal tea.

"This cabin used to belong to Harper Reed, an old friend of mine," he said. "He was from Devon and went to school at Clifton College in Bristol, where he got a good education. But many of those Britishers had trouble with their lungs, and the doctors told him to go to a dry climate or get out to the colonies."

As we looked around the room, we realized that it had changed little since Harper died. We could see into the workshop across a small porch. Old tools lay on the bench, and useful things were tied in linen bags hanging from the rafters.

"Harper came to Canada in about 1902 after being rejected on medical grounds for service in the South African War." said Gerry, continuing his saga. "After two years, he came to the Alaska Panhandle and got a job with a party surveying the 141st meridian to the Arctic near Herschel Island off the Yukon's north coast: the boundary between Canada and the United States. Harper got on well with the chief surveyor who hired him every summer season until 1912."

At the outbreak of World War I, Harper Reed joined the 6th Canadian Field Company Engineers and was promoted to captain. He applied unsuccessfully to join the North Russian Expeditionary Force, but instead was sent to the front lines in France. After the war, he led a detachment of Canadian Sappers in the Victory Parade. Harper once told Gerry that "In this engagement, I lost four fully equipped Sappers who were snatched from the ranks by certain ladies of London City and were never seen again."

Harper was reported "wounded, later deceased and interred in Ontario." On returning to Canada, he had to prove his identity. He gravitated to Wrangell, Alaska, bought a motorized river boat, and prospected up the Stikine River. In 1928, the Indian Agent in Telegraph Creek died suddenly of a heart attack. Ottawa needed a quick replacement and offered Harper the job of administering one of the largest native districts in British Columbia, which included Atlin. He spent the next fifteen years wandering through the region and always slept on his river boat during inspection tours rather than accepting hospitality from Hudson's Bay Company managers, of whom he had a poor opinion.

"He fell in love with Atlin," said Gerry. "Same as the rest of us."

A cantankerous bachelor, Harper annotated the margins of all his books and papers with acerbic comments. Gerry showed us a copy of Guy Lawrence's book *40 Years on the Yukon Telegraph*, which describes the lives of linemen in isolated cabins set about fifty kilometres apart along the Telegraph Trail. The 3,000 kilometre trail was built in 1899 to link the gold fields of the Klondike with southern Canada — the greatest wilderness undertaking of the era. It cost several million dollars and served the nation for half a century. The dedication in the book reads: *This book is dedicated in tribute to the employees of the old Yukon Telegraph Line many of whom gave their lives to maintain the Service.*

Appended to this dedication in Harper's copy, written in spidery handwriting was: "Excepting Joe Hicks Nahlin, old Moose McKay & one or two others, the gang were a squaw-chasing (Moonshine Maggie and Gunny Sack Mary) bunch of so-called white trappers, bootleggers & no-good trouble makers. H.R."

"Back in Telegraph Creek," said Gerry Andrews, "Harper heard from a fisherman in Wrangell that the Grand Pacific Glacier had receded to inside the Canadian boundary. This meant there was tidewater for about a quarter of a mile inside Canada at the head of Tarr Inlet on the west arm of Glacier Bay."

He reported this to Ottawa because it implied the prospect of a deep-water port for the northwest corner of British Columbia. Such a facility had previously been denied due to the settlement of the 1904 Boundary Commission. Harper consulted Gerry, who drew up a plan to build a road from the Haines Highway along the Tatshenshini Valley to the Melburn Glacier and then down the Grand Pacific Glacier to Tarr Inlet. The glacial moraines had abundant gravel for road construction. Gerry thought it possible to build a nuclear power plant to melt the toe of the Grand Pacific Glacier to prevent it from surging forward into American territory. If the glacier did advance it would destroy Canadian foreshore and any chance of a deep-water harbour.

Harper Reed and guide. *(Yukon Archives/Atlin Historical Society Collection, No. 9726)*

Sadly the concept died, but it resurfaces every decade or so only to sink once again into obscurity. Perhaps one day it will become viable, and Gerry will be vindicated.

Harper Reed retired to Atlin, bought the house next door to ours, and tacked on a small cabin as a guest wing. He lived there for a dozen years, but finally went into a nursing home in Victoria. When he died, he left Gerry all his property: his cabin, the dock at the bottom of Rant Avenue, and several lots in town. A memorial erected in Atlin's Pioneer Cemetery reads: "Harper Reed, Gentleman Adventurer — 1878-1965." Others have labelled this controversial personality as "an adventurer, but no gentleman."

Gerry paused in his story, sipped tea, relit his pipe, and went on. "Harper wrote a note to me shortly before he died. It read, 'After all that talk about packing dogs over to Herschel Island, they offered to give me a FRGS (Fellowship of the Royal Geographical Society), and I turned it down. But they did make me scribble

my name under Roald Amundsen's.'" Further conversation with
Gerry revealed the coincidence that, along with Harper Reed, both
he and I are also Fellows of the RGS.

Having passed the better part of an hour over tea, Sarah caught
my eye and indicated that it was time to go. As we rose, Gerry said,
"Let me show you something special." He led us across the rough
grass in front of the cabin, knelt down, and parted the leaves of a
small Manitoba split-leaf maple tree. An inscription, stamped on a
piece of copper wrapped around a post, read:

> R.I.P.
> Here lies
> AH–TE–HA
> Tahltan Bear Dog
> of Telegraph Creek
> with his pal
> ANGUS SCOTTY
> killed fighting great odds
> Fall 1952
> Beware
> Let sleeping dogs lie
> Under this maple tree
> they rest in peace HR

I cannot elaborate on "killed fighting great odds," but it brings
to mind an image of a plucky little dog taking on a grizzly bear.
The name of the breed comes from Tahltan, a village at the junction of the Stikine and Tahltan Rivers, ten kilometres upstream from
Telegraph Creek. Tahltan Bear Dogs mated once a year and had one
to four pups that the bitch would kill if threatened. Standing twenty
centimetres high at the shoulder, a bear dog weighed less than ten
kilograms. The foxy head had a pointed, grizzled white muzzle and

large forward-pointing prick ears. The coat was a mix of white with black or grey-blue hair, and the brush tail was short and stubby.

Bear dogs could find a den through deep snow and were trained to hunt bears by nipping them in the flanks and chasing them up trees. Then they yelped in a high-pitched staccato bark like a coyote, darting and lunging at the bear and holding it at bay until the hunter arrived. Indians would prime their dogs two days before a hunt in a sort of ritual bleeding by stabbing them in the rump with the fibula of a fox or wolf.

"In the old days when hunting was done with bows and arrows," John Carlick, a Taku Tlingit, told Gerry Andrews, "They would keep us alive, chasing rabbits and putting up grouse and ptarmigan. But modern rifles put bear dogs out of business."

Now the Tahltan Bear Dog is extinct for want of a mating pair. The memorial in Gerry's garden, and photos of the last pure-bred dog, Iskut, are scant reminders of a courageous breed.

On the wall beside Gerry's table, a large-scale map of the Atlin town site was marked with coloured pins and flags bearing the names of the householders.

"That map keeps me up-to-date with everyone," Gerry chuckled. Then he turned to the large composite map that covered one entire wall and included the area of southeast Alaska, Yukon's southern lakes, and northwest British Columbia — the region where the Klondike gold rush happened and of which the Atlin rush was an offshoot.

"To fully appreciate what happened in Atlin," he said, "it's helpful to understand the Klondike."

From Gerry's stories and my own research, I was able to piece together a picture of the massive migration of miners and hangers-on that occurred at the turn of the century.

The town of Skagway lies a half-hour flight by small plane from Atlin across the glaciers of the Juneau Icecap, part of the coastal mountain range. In 1898, Taiya Inlet, at the head of the Lynn Canal, was the trail head for gold seekers taking the seaward route from Seattle and Vancouver and heading for Dawson City and the Klondike gold fields. The mother lode of Yukon gold was also approached from Nome, Alaska, on the Bering Sea, by travelling upstream on the Yukon River. A less popular route from northern Alberta and British Columbia came through the Peace River country.

Prospectors approaching from the Pacific first had to cross the Chilkoot Pass, a 1,500-metre-high gap in the Coast Range. Their lust for gold was matched by their ineptitude in mountains and their heavy, clumsy gear. Before allowing the stampeders into the Yukon, North West Mounted Police (NWMP) posted on the Chilkoot Summit checked to be sure that they carried a grubstake of food and supplies enough to last a year. If not, they were turned back. Among the discarded junk still lying on the summit is a pile of collapsible canvas boats rejected by the police. On the shores of Bennett Lake, 25 kilometres beyond the pass, men used trees to build scows and rafts on which to sail, row, or float down river to Dawson. Old photos show the landscape denuded of trees, as though shaven bald with a razor.

As soon as the ice went out, the stampeders set off from Bennett Lake toward Carcross (Caribou Crossing). The lower part of Tagish Lake narrows into a short river where another NWMP post checked the flotilla through and registered the names of all passers. At the north end of Marsh Lake, where the southern Yukon lakes and waterways converge like the spokes of a wheel, they reached the start of the Yukon River.

Whitehorse, the highest navigable point on the Yukon River, became the communication hub of the territory. Today, the Alaska Highway and all the major roads of the territory radiate from this city. Many flimsy craft that survived violent storms on the Southern Lakes were abandoned at Canyon City, just upriver of Miles Canyon. There, a 200-metre-long ravine cut through high basalt cliffs, and the river eddied into several giant whirlpools. Then it picked up speed and bounced through the white water of the Whitehorse Rapids.

Wise landlubbers disembarked at Canyon City and put their gear on cars that were hauled by horses along a tramway made of logs laid lengthwise. Jack London worked for a season piloting boats through the rapids to Whitehorse and incorporated his experiences in his stories. At the Whitehorse shipyards, passengers could buy tickets on the flat-bottomed paddle-wheelers bound for the Klondike.

The White Pass & Yukon Route was founded in May 1898 by "Big Mike" Heney. He designed a railway from Skagway to cross the Coast Mountains by way of the White Pass, just east of the Chilkoot Pass. Sir Thomas Tancrede, a financier from England, put up the $10 million to pay for the project.

One railroad construction gang started from Skagway and climbed 34 kilometres to the summit at 1,003 metres. The average gradient was 2.6 percent (the maximum gradient was four percent). Another gang worked in the other direction. A golden spike was driven at Carcross where the two gangs finished the line.

When gold was struck on Pine Creek near Atlin, in 1900, four years after the Klondike discovery, 13,000 White Pass & Yukon Route workers shouldered the company's picks and shovels and headed east to seek their fortunes. News of the Atlin strike filtered through to Skagway and camps along the Chilkoot Trail, where miners were heading towards the Yukon River. Attracted by the shorter and more appealing trail to Atlin, many miners and hangers-on turned right at Log Cabin to try their luck on the Pine, Spruce, McKee, Ruby, Boulder, and Otter Creeks.

Map contours show low land all the way east from Log Cabin and the glacial lakes around Fraser. The land rises slightly between Tepee Peak and Mount Lawson and then drops towards Fantail Lake, which drains into the Taku Arm of Tagish Lake at Golden Gate. Opposite, Graham Inlet leads to Taku Landing and the mouth of the Atlinto River. In winter, it is comparatively easy to travel across the frozen lakes, and so this route became the portal to Atlin's offshoot gold rush. Atlin's population swelled to 10,000 people, and the town boomed until 1910. Then it dwindled, as gold rush towns will, to a few hundred persons.

After the gold rush, Americans from the Lower 48 discovered Alaska as a place for vacations, and Atlin became a fashionable destination for tourists. Boats that brought miners in 1898 were replaced by cruise ships out of San Francisco and Seattle. These sailed up the Inland Passage among the multitude of offshore islands along the coast of British Columbia and the Alaska Panhandle. At this point in its history, Skagway, once terrorized by the gangster Soapy Smith and his band of hoodlums, was a one-horse town with a single main street lined with false-fronted houses and boardwalks.

Tourists bent on visiting Atlin disembarked at Skagway and took the train to Carcross. They rode one of the world's most spectacular narrow gauge railways on which they either sat facing outwards in comfortable coaches, or stood on open platforms at either end or in a caboose at the rear. Jagged alpine mountains rose on both sides as the track switch backed through forest and gorge and meandered into side valleys to gain height. The land at the summit of the White Pass is an atavistic moonscape with countless kettle lakes and rolling humpback glacial moraines. The latter are barren except for juniper and willow scrub. Over the top, the railway track angles gradually down to the old refuelling station at Fraser, where the Canadian Customs post now stands. Nearby, at Log Cabin, the railway track and the modern road cross and part.

Soon after arriving in the Yukon, our family took the train to Skagway and hiked back over the Chilkoot Pass to Bennett. This three or four day expedition passes through wild scenery of coastal rain forest, glaciated mountains, and arid alpine uplands. The trail is littered with ancient tin cans, old boots, and pieces of discarded gear — the detritus of gold rush history. Those early pioneers, beset by cold, hunger, and discomfort, tenaciously hauled huge pieces of heavy gold-mining machinery across the mountains.

Bennett was the first place the railway met the waters at the head of navigation on the Yukon River system. The railway hugs the edge of Lake Bennett all the way to Carcross, where an iron girder bridge spans a short river that flows into Tagish Lake. The Indian village is on the east bank, and on the west the train station stands across from the Caribou Hotel and Matthew Watson's general store.

After 1917, tourists heading for Atlin transferred to the paddle-steamer Tutshi, which was docked at Carcross against pilings in the river bank below the train station. Near that spot, the steamer was eventually hauled up on ways and restored as an historic site, but she was reduced to a shell by arson in 1989. The Tutshi, with a full complement of passengers and crew, would huff and puff into the meandering channel that leads through the mud flats between Nares and Montana Mountain. Level with Bove Island, a stiff breeze issues from Windy Arm.

Past Ten Mile Point, the Taku Arm of Tagish Lake turns south for seventy kilometres. To the east lies Talaha Bay, where the dog sled trail from Carcross and Striker's Pass leads to Moose Arm and then across a neck of land to Atlin Lake. At Golden Gate, the Taku Arm of Tagish Lake narrows and forms, with Fantail Lake and Graham Inlet, the arms of a cross. At the head of Graham Inlet is Taku Landing, where a steamer dock, a train station and a few sheds were the start of the Atlin Short Line Railway. It carried the passengers four kilometres to Scotia Bay, where they transferred to a boat bound for Atlin.

Fascinating though Gerry's stories were, I had to get on with the renovations to the cabin. I built a two-tier bunk across the end of the narrow bedroom — queen size for Sarah and me below and head-to-toe for the children above. It was like those bunks found in the Alpine climbing huts of my youth. A ladder nailed to the wall gave access to the top bunk, which had about a metre of headroom.

Womb-like on a stormy evening, it was a place for the children to escape and enjoy reading with only a teddy bear for company. Here, they could feast on comics, which they were not allowed to read in Whitehorse.

To the right of the door was a rack of shelves, one labelled for each member of the family. I later discovered that I had narrowly missed drilling through the main power cable when passing the supporting bracket for the shelf through the kitchen wall. Sarah was the designer and planner; I was the labourer. Her appliqué moose and birds brightened the walls, and she hung some pictures. Queen Victoria stared down, very unamused, from one of them.

Next we tackled the sitting room. Sarah upholstered foam cushions for a bench where the bathroom once stood. We left the original dresser intact. I demolished the bathroom by taking down a framed wall in a corner of the sitting room. This left a scar on the ceiling that I covered with pine board and moulding.

I graduated from crudely hammering four-inch nails to mortising joints and corners. I wanted to refine my skills — plastic surgery in contrast to orthopaedics, but without the blood. There was no plumbing to dismantle, but the elegant bath had brass-bossed taps. We guessed that Ira heated water on the wood stove and used buckets to fill his weekly bath. Perhaps he dreamed of someday building a proper bathroom.

We moved the bathtub outside into the yard. Bruce Johnson, a dog musher whose homestead was beside the Atlinto River, admired it covetously as a water trough for his horses and racing dogs. We gave it to him and last saw it in the bottom of his freighter canoe as he headed across the lake into the teeth of a mounting storm. With the tub as ballast, Bruce needed all his boatman's skill, because the canoe had perilously little freeboard.

We put windows into the outside porch facing the lake and moved the door round to the side.

"There's a pile of timber cluttering my yard," said Dick Sneigocki, owner of the Atlin Trading Post, when I was telling him of my carpentry projects. "It's tongue-and-groove that came out of the old police station. It's probably been there more than half a century. Take it all away if you want."

The lumber had lain outside in all weathers, yet each board was still straight and every tongue fitted every groove. We clad the interior of the porch and still had some timber left over. I built a desk with a wide working surface that extended the full width of the room. The tabletop and seat were the same size and slid onto battens on the wall. Laid side-by-side they made a double bed. By lifting our heads off the pillow, Sarah and I can look out over the lake and mountains when we sleep there in summer.

The cabin has become a repository for knickknacks we covet. One wall behind the table is covered with a hand-sewn Nova Scotia quilt in a comfortable blend of Acadian pink, light blue, and yellow. Sarah's appliqué of birds against a vermilion background brightens the wall above the counter. Nailed to the wall is a stove door that we found rusting in a hedgerow beside our cottage in Wales. Sarah's father cleaned it and revealed an embossed fleur-de-lys and Queen Caroline's head.

Hanging above the window are ladles and a strainer that were beaten out of aluminum by a Tibetan metal smith we met on our family journey across Bhutan. A row of cast-iron cooking pots hangs above the stove. On the windowsills stand two oil lamps, a blue glass bottle picked up at Discovery Mine, the side of a box marked "Giant Gelatin" and two prospectors' stake post markers. Sarah's stuffed appliqué moose hangs beside a porcelain mermaid with oversized busts, made by Judith in grade two, and a cross-stitch embroidery of the cabin by Lucy.

With the cabin partly renovated, we began to explore our environs and meet more of our neighbours. Maureen Morris rented the house to our right for her sculpture workshop. Peeling paint revealed weathered shiplap walls that had once been yellow with green trim, but hadn't seen a lick of paint for many years. The house, built at the same time as ours, had a front door porch flanked by windows. A pile of firewood lay outside beside a beat-up skidoo.

Maureen came to Atlin seeking a quiet life away from Vancouver where she had attended art school.

"I used to carve in jade," she said. "Then one day, I noticed a neighbour's dog chewing on a piece of moose antler. I asked to experiment with it and discovered that my jade-carving equipment worked well on bone. So, with a steady supply of raw material, I decided to change my carving medium to bone antler."

Her long, delicate fingers work on moose and caribou antler using a high-speed drill — far removed from her traditional sculptor's chisel and mallet. She wears coveralls and a mask, because the air in her workshop is laden with thick bone dust. While working, her waist-length, coppery hair is wound into a turban on the crown of her head. She works under bright light, and the grinding wheel emits a high-pitched whine — not the peaceful ambiance one usually associates with an artist's studio.

Trappers going into the bush will often give Maureen cast-off antlers that she stores in a pile on the roof of her back porch. Caribou antler has tones of rich pink, mustard, and copper-brown. The bone is channelled by veins coursing under the velvet, and the cut bone shows a rough lattice skeleton. Maureen started carving images of the flocks of little gray birds that come to Atlin in spring and stay most of the summer. Then she became more adventurous and turned to larger mythical birds with long curved necks and graceful bodies.

With the wide plates from moose antlers she carves masks that are based on native Indian designs. The frilled roots of antlers she turns into owls' feet, and from the gently curved lines of the fingers at the ends of the horn she makes elegant swans and herons. Now she has moved to a new home at the other end of town, and her workshop is better lit and ventilated. We miss being able to drop by on our way back from the store across the street to watch her work.

The store was once a "sporting house" (euphemism for brothel) situated on the road to Discovery just past Halfway House near the Pine Creek Bridge. It was later moved down to Atlin. Ross Peebler, a former miner, trapper, and mail dog-team driver, became the storekeeper and also ran it also as a café. When Teresa Hunt bought the store she named it The Food Basket and erected an inviting sign that shows a samovar and a promise of "tea always on the boil."

When we arrived in Atlin, Bob Fassell, a large man with tattoos on his hands, lived in the three-storey house kitty-corner to us. His fence posts were carved and poker-burned in weird shapes, and he habitually wore black leather, which gave him a spooky mien. Once on a sailing trip to Sloko Inlet, we found a strange gravestone carved by Fassell with his own name on it.

One warm Easter day a few years ago, the Fassell's five-year-old son, Carlos, unnoticed by people flying kites in front of town, went galloping off down the lake ice on his hobbyhorse. News of the boy's disappearance ricocheted around town and, with less than an hour of daylight, a plane took off, skiers started down the lake, and children scoured the islands in front of town. Carlos was found safe 10 kilometres away, but the incident proved that the whole town could be mobilized in a hurry. The former Fassell house is now the Fireweed Inn, a comfortable bed and breakfast.

A small house directly across the street from us, a composite of three cabins from Spruce Creek, had lain empty for years. One day, Kathy and Jack Weltzin, an American couple with three children, moved in. They had driven down the Alaska Highway from Anchorage to camp and explore Atlin for a few days. They bought the house on sight and Jack, a retired schoolteacher and jack of all trades, began to renovate it. His yard was a rummager's delight; he hoarded every scrap of metal or wood against a day it might come in handy. Kathy was the interior planner and fixer; Jack the heavy construction man — roles much like Sarah's and mine.

The Weltzins worked at the cabin all that first summer. They built a large porch out back and an extra bedroom. Then Jack put a second storey on top of the old roof with a French window opening from the master bedroom onto a balcony. Kathy tore down the thin plasterboard wall covering in the kitchen and found some newspapers dated 1901 stuffed into the wall space for insulation. We often crossed the street in idle moments, leaned on the fence to examine their latest project, and reminisced over our own rebuilding.

Kathy's kindly eyes shine out of round granny glasses. She works in alcohol education, as Sarah used to do, and runs a program in a middle grade school in Juneau — now their winter home. Jack was powerfully built with fair curly hair and a bushy beard. The Weltzins, the Merrys, and we are about the same age and, when we met, our kids were variously going through the same taxing stages of adolescence. So discussing their teenage tribulations brought much mutual comfort. Peter Ustinov writes in his autobiography, *Dear Me*, "I have forgotten what it was like to be young. I do remember, however, that being young is difficult enough to deserve my greatest respect."

One day, Kathy came over to our house full of excitement. "I've just ripped up the lino and found fir floorboards right through the house," she said. "I bet your floors are the same."

We levered away the corner of the butt-end burned, chocolate-brown linoleum that was so old and stiff it cracked with each pry of the crowbar. Kathy was correct, so we tore up the linoleum throughout the house and found fir boards that were pristine everywhere except under where Ira Bennett's sink had stood.

We rented a heavy-duty rotary sanding machine in Whitehorse and returned the next weekend to sand the floors. It was a tricky job; if one lingered too long in one place the rotating disc of the heavy sander dug in and made circular scars on the wood. Our eyes and lungs were clogged with fine sawdust, which we allowed to settle before thoroughly vacuuming the house. Then we painted the

Sarah taking a well
deserved break.

first coat of varnish on the floors and went camping at Warm Bay
for the weekend in order to let it dry. Before leaving Atlin on Sunday evening, we painted a second coat, which we left to harden.
The cabin had became suddenly brighter.

Rebuilding the cabin took most of the first summer. By working most weekends, the little house became comfortable and in fair
order. Hard work though it was, each weekend brought a new
challenge. Sarah was busy with needle and thread, my carpentry
improved, and soon we had the deep satisfaction of being able to
live there comfortably. The children were happy to be in the centre of town. They were close to the store and to their friends, and
they could ride their bikes unhindered by traffic. An isolated cabin
away in the bush, though an adult idyll, was not their idea of fun.

With the approaching fall in mind, I hired Jim Wallis, who con-
tracted heavy equipment to placer miners, to shore up the basement. Parts of the wooden foundation were rotting after fifty or

more years in the ground. He dug a channel with his back hoe to expose and strengthen the north wall. Bo Eriksen, a Swedish carpenter, replaced the floor joists with heavy timbers and poured concrete around their footings. He cemented the tamped earth basement floor to protect it from sparks and cribbed the legs of the furnace.

All was not skookum in the basement, however. Every spring, as water seeped out of the frozen ground, it flooded and soaked any logs still stored there. We pumped it out with an electrical sump pump and a length of hose that we borrowed from the fire hall.

By the end of August, when poplar, willows and aspens change to yellow and gold among the dark green spruce, a paint job had brightened the former insipid pale green walls to a more robust cobalt blue. Sarah chose white for the window casings, door surrounds, and corner trim. With new black roof tiles, our cabin was transformed. Returning to Whitehorse as another weekend drew to a close, I resented medical work for interfering with the joy of rough wood building.

Pearl Avenue

Each weekend, we made the two-hour drive from Whitehorse to the end of the Atlin Road. Atlin was a destination loaded with anticipation of new discoveries, especially for our children who grew to identify more and more with the place. Because much of Atlin's charm lies in its historical buildings, we strove to make the cabin comfortable without destroying its original appearance.

To allow the reader to savour some of the town's rich history, let's take a stroll down Pearl Avenue, where some of Atlin's most historic buildings still stand. It cuts east-west across the middle of town, from the liquor store to the lake — a distance of some two hundred metres. As we examine Atlin's history, we must remember that fires swept through the town in 1914 and 1916, devastating all but a few buildings on the perimeter. Among the buildings that escaped the flames are the Courthouse, the Anglican Church, and the school.

A memorial to these fires is the hand pump that stands under a weather shelter outside the fire hall on the corner of Pearl and Second. This manual fire pump and water carrier, repainted royal red with gold lettering, was shipped to Atlin from Portland, Oregon in 1901. It was used in both serious fires, and was described by a witness as *a back-breaking hand pump which eight men worked by raising and lowering long bars on each side. They worked in relays on the pump, and men, women, and children formed a chain to the lake and passed buckets. It was astonishing how little water arrived in a bucket after some 80 people had passed it frantically from hand to hand.*

The 1916 fire started in the Royal Hotel. An employee was frying bacon on the stove at the same time as some workmen were boiling tar for repairing the roof. The bacon caught alight and, while trying to carry it outside, she dropped flaming fat on the floor, where it ignited the tar. The resulting fire burnt down most of the town. A photo in the Atlin Museum shows Jules Eggert standing beside his walk-in safe. It lay in the midst of the burned ruins of his store, surrounded by the fire-ravaged town. He found a case of frozen butter intact inside the safe.

When the fire was under control, the saloon owners passed around free drinks to exhausted firemen from the barrels of whiskey that had been saved. Unfortunately, a watchman, posted to oversee the smouldering ruins, indulged in the whiskey, and the wind fanned the embers into flames that destroyed another nine houses. So most of the buildings that stand in Atlin today were built after 1916.

At the top end of Pearl Avenue, the liquor store resembles a half-timbered barn. A safe stands in one corner with ornate landscape vignettes painted on brass-handled doors. Inside is written:

This safe was sold on February 22nd 1899 to the British Columbia Government and shipped to Mr. J. D. Graham, Government Agent in Atlin B.C. It is a Model 17 safe and the painting on the front was done by Taylor, craftsman of that time.

Glen McKenzie, the manager, keeps a connoisseur's selection of wine on the shelves. He has assumed the mantle of the local fish-

The morning after the disastrous fire of 1914. *(Yukon Archives/Atlin Historical Society Collection, p.1139)*

ing guru and divulges to a chosen few the best places in the lake to find trout.

Across the street, drawing the eye from every corner of town, is the large and imposing old government building, which is known as the Courthouse. Designed by Atlin architect Edward Garden, it was built of imported fir by a local contractor. Originally it stood a block away on Third Street, the site of the present Red Cross Outpost Hospital, but it was moved in 1955. The building appears higher than its two storeys because of a tall tower that has a widow's walk around the base and a flagpole atop. Dormer windows in the steep-pitched mansard roof light the second storey.

When the Courthouse opened in 1900, it was painted beige with boot-brown trim. It is now restored in the same colours and sits on a square base with a wide staircase leading to a covered porch and double front doors. As a B.C. government administration building, the courthouse originally housed the court, quarters for the

District Magistrate, and offices for the Gold Commissioner, the Registrar of Claims, and the Deputy Mining Recorder.

To the left of a high-ceilinged hallway are the judges' chambers and the spacious courtroom, both still used for their original purpose (Atlin is on the Province of British Columbia northern outposts court circuit). A royal coat-of-arms hangs above the judge's bench. A balustraded platform separates it from a foot-scuffed witness podium and a kidney-shaped lawyer's desk. The latter is said to have been a blackjack dealer's table in a saloon in nearby Discovery City. The chambers are bare except for a chaise longue, where the judge can stretch out between cases (although the workload on the northern circuit is never too arduous).

Across the hall from the courtroom were offices that now house the town library and art gallery. A wide graceful staircase climbs to the floor above, once the living quarters of the Gold Commissioner and now adult education classrooms of Northern Lights College. The basement once contained the dormitory for junior clerks and, in winter, when it was too cold to use the jail house, the police lockup. One prisoner reported that "Being in jail here consists of having the run of the cop's house, bringing him coffee in bed in the morning, and cooking his meals".

Apart from a few petty crimes, Atlin was fairly law-abiding at the turn of the century compared with nearby Skagway, so the Courthouse didn't see much action over the years. The biggest task for the police lay in controlling gambling in the hotels and the liquor trade in the "sporting houses."

Alcohol has always been a problem in mining towns and has occasionally resulted in shootings. In 1899, Leninga, a Swede, attempted to shoot a man. He resisted arrest for three days, but was eventually caught and put in jail pending the death or recovery of the victim. He escaped and was never seen again. In the same year a stagecoach, carrying passengers on the road to Discovery, was held up at gun point by masked gunmen. The passengers delivered up their cash to the amount of $3.56. One resourceful person, who

The Discovery gaol, Masonic Lodge and town clock on Pearl Avenue.

had a bag of gold dust in his pocket, jumped out of the door and escaped into the bush.

Guns are still much in evidence today, as we discovered on our first Christmas Eve in Atlin. The RCMP called at the cabin as Sarah was trying to fit a large turkey into our small wood stove oven. The children and I were setting up a balsam fir that we had just cut down beside the Warm Bay Road — an act which was illegal within ten metres of the road.

"Excuse me bothering you, Doctor," said the officer, "but there's been some trouble with a shooting. Could you come down to the detachment and talk to the person in custody."

In the cell, I found a distraught young woman, pale and tear-stained. After a squabble, she had taken a rifle from her cabin, re-turned to the garage shop where her partner was working, and let fly through the open doors. Fortunately the bullet hit the back wall of the shed, narrowly missing her target who wrested the gun from her.

The police wanted to release her for the holiday under my recognizance. I willingly agreed, and two hours later I returned to the cabin. Our three ravenous children were annoyed at their Christmas being so disturbed.

"Where have you been, Dad?" grouched Judith. "We're starving. And it's Christmas too."

"Sorry, guys, but there's been a shooting," I replied.

"What do they want guns for, anyway?" asked Adam. "I thought they were meant to keep them locked up."

"Mostly they're for hunting," I said. "But guns also kill people."

This led to a vigorous discussion about the use of guns, with which I was singularly unfamiliar. It also served as a vivid lesson to us all of their dangers.

Court is an important social event in the life of a small town where everyone knows everyone else's business, rumour may supplant fact, and the administration of justice, as of medicine, may take an unusual turn. Judges usually come from southern British Columbia, many hundreds of kilometres away, but in an emergency a judge from the Yukon may substitute.

One winter's day in 1978, Judge Dennis O'Connor, the senior magistrate for the Yukon, was asked by the Atlin RCMP to arraign on a charge of arson, a person who had allegedly set fire to a chicken farm after a domestic dispute. On the morning of court, the thermometer read 40 degrees below zero in Whitehorse.

To cut travel time and to diminish the risk of being stranded, Judge O'Connor called the RCMP corporal in Atlin and suggested meeting at the survival shelter about halfway down the Atlin Road. Because Atlin is just inside the border of British Columbia, provincial law would apply. The shelter is like a box with a sloping lean-to roof, a door, and a tiny window; inside, there is enough room for a bed, a small tin Yukon wood stove, and a table and chair.

The Atlin Mountie and the prisoner arrived first. Together they lit the stove with wood brought in the police truck and hung a picture of the Queen beside a Canadian flag pinned to the wall. The judge set off from Whitehorse in company with the court reporter and arrived a few minutes after the appointed time of ten o'clock. He took his place at the rickety table, and the prisoner sat on bare bedsprings; squirrels had eaten the mattress.

"Prisoner rise," ordered the Mountie, who then read out the charge.

"Have you anything to say?" asked the judge. Not wishing to speak, the prisoner was scheduled to appear in court at a later date. Court was formally adjourned, and the judge walked ponderously back to his vehicle, the engine of which was still running to prevent the cab from freezing. Judge and Mountie drove off in opposite directions along the snowy road that crunched and squeaked in the still, cold air.

Behind the Courthouse sits the original one-room schoolhouse, built in 1902 and used as a school until 1968. Then it became the museum and repository of the Atlin Historical Society archives, a remarkable collection for so small a town. Parked around the yard is machinery from the early days: steam diggers, a Caterpillar bulldozer, a horse-drawn snowplough, sleighs, and several old boats. Opposite the school is Jack Green's house, once part of the old Pine Creek Hotel at Discovery.

Kitty-corner stands St. Martin's Anglican church. Built in 1901, this is the oldest building in Atlin. Adjacent to the Courthouse is the Pyramid. This building, constructed out of vertical logs, was erected as a spiritual healing centre by Dr. Don Branigan, maverick Mayor of Whitehorse and controversial practitioner of alternative medicine.

On the corner of Second Street stands the fire hall, its false front painted orange-brown. The Atlin Volunteer Fire Department, part of the social fabric of the town, was licked into shape by Wayne

Merry in the 1970s. Using his experience in emergency rescue and administration, gained from working in the U.S. Parks Service at Denali, he organized the fire hall, acquired new trucks, and found space for the ambulance. The fire crew practices every Monday at 7.30 p.m., when sirens howl over the town, crews scurry to their tasks, and townspeople are reminded that they are protected by willing and competent volunteers.

The old Telegraph Office, a magisterial building similar in style and size to the Courthouse, stood on the corner of Pearl and Second, but was destroyed in the 1914 fire. Now all that remains is an empty grassy plot. Bob Nelson, postmaster for twenty-four years, went to France in 1916 to fight with the 72nd Battalion along with Norman Fisher and other men from Atlin. Louis Schulz, a merchant, accompanied them to Carcross on the Tagish Lake sternwheeler *Scotia*. He returned to find Atlin burned to the ground.

Of the thirteen men who went overseas to the war, only three returned. One who didn't was Billy Clarke. When in the trenches in France, he asked Bob Nelson to look after his wife should he not survive. Nelson returned to Vancouver to carry out his promise and subsequently married Clarke's widow. He took on her four children and they had three more of their own.

Moving down the hill, on the left is Eggert's jewellery store, decorated with sunrise angle-fillers above a gable and cornice. It was moved to Atlin from Discovery by John Noland and his team of horses in the 1920s to replace buildings destroyed in the great fires. Jules Eggert, a Swiss watchmaker lured north by the gold rush, crossed the Chilkoot Pass and found his way to Atlin. His jewellery became famous: teaspoons with gold nuggets soldered to the handle, gold-plated brooches of lizards and frogs with turquoise eyes, and necklaces with nuggets strung on a two-metre chain.

After Eggert moved to a second location at the corner of Pearl Avenue and First Street, the old Discovery store was never used as a jewellers again. It was rented to Jenny Bender, reputedly a "sport" in her youth who later became respectable. She ran a barber shop, outside of which hung a red and white candy-striped pole (representing the blood and bandages of the barber surgeons). Chickens strutted around clients' feet. Jenny lived upstairs in winter and downstairs in summer and had her piano moved according to the seasons by way of a narrow outside staircase. She had two large dogs tied up beside the house by day and took them upstairs at night. Each summer, tiny Jenny travelled to her mining claims on Wilson Creek using a wooden dog cart. When she died, the old store was run as a café and then as a photographer's shop.

Opposite the old Discovery store stands the Globe Theatre, built in 1917 for Edwin W. Pillman: entrepreneur, store owner, outfitter, market gardener, and latterly, mortician. Atlin children, who hung out in his store just below the theatre to read comics or leave messages for friends, knew him as Pills. His moustache hid a harelip, and a dental plate closed a cleft palate which gave his speech a nasal twang that only the kids could understand. Children used to creep into the store and, despite the clang of the doorbell, Pills would sit in his chair behind the store counter pretending to be asleep. They tied Pills to his chair, and then he would wake up and scare them.

A peep-hole opened through to the sitting room in the back of the store so that Mrs. Ethel Lavinia Pillman could talk to her husband. She wore high-buttoned boots long after they went out of fashion; some say she was buried in them. Pills liked to have a little flutter every day in the bar of the Northern Hotel, where he placed a dollar bet — just one dollar — at roulette, blackjack, or poker.

The Globe Theatre had a stage at one end with wings and entrances from both sides and a barrel-vaulted ceiling of steam-bent pine boards. The hall was used for movies and magic lantern shows and Christmas concerts, New Year dances, and other community functions. A newly-ordered pianola, while being unloaded from the boat, slipped off the gangplank and fell into the lake. They dried it out, and it worked adequately for many years.

Cyril James got free admission to the movies as reward for running around town clanging a bell to announce show time.

"Pills operated the hand-crank projector," Cyril told me when I visited him just before he died, "but when he got sleepy the film began to drag and the kids would holler at him. He'd jerk to, speed up the film, and soon the horses would dash across the screen. Pills would put a sign up on the screen reading, 'Just one moment, please,' but it invariably stayed up twenty minutes or more. Six months after talkies came out, he had one in Atlin, but the film was all mixed up; horses talked instead of people."

Touring professional boxers turned up in Atlin to challenge all comers, so fights were staged in the Globe Theatre. The professionals rarely beat local Atlin miners who were fit from squirming into narrow underground tunnels. Once, a touring American pugilist insulted a mulatto sporting girl. Cyril James, a handy boxer in his youth, fancied the girl, so he challenged the visitor to a fight in front of eighty miners gathered in the fenced garden of the hotel.

"Instead of proper boxing gloves, they wrapped towels round our fists," said Cyril. "We kept them in place with safety pins. In the second round, the professional worked his pins loose and almost knocked me out. Before the next round, my second undid my safety pins. The towels came off, and I knocked the boxer cold with my bare fist."

Legend has it that Henry Taku Jack once took on, and beat, a burly Scottish prizefighter who had called him "an Indian S.O.B."

Children often tobogganed down the hill outside the Globe Theatre — coasting, as it was known. One day, Pillman was hauling a sled-load of firewood from his woodpile on the corner near his the store. The road was icy all the way to the lake, but Pillman started down anyway. He gained speed, lost control, and just kept on going past the store.

"Watcha doin', Pills?" shouted Cyril, who was standing outside.

"Just coastin'," replied Pillman, who didn't stop until he was well out on the lake ice.

Pillman was into any business venture that would make money. Before coming to Atlin he ran stores in Skagway, Dyea, and at the O'Donnell River. Then he turned his hand to the lucrative mortician business, using a hearse pulled by his faithful old horse, Beth. He put an advertisement in the newspaper:

Funeral Director & Embalmer. Bodies embalmed for shipment a speciality. Orders on short notice. All kinds of funeral supplies at reasonable rates.

Unfortunately, Pillman lost business because of his aggressive marketing. Bruce Morton, set up a morgue down by the wharf, and townsfolk transferred their loyalty to him because he was reputed to be more respectful with the bodies than his rival. Angus Macdonald, a miner who was in the hospital after a mine cave-in on Boulder Creek, caught Pillman peeking through the windows of the hospital to check for potential customers.

"Not yet, old Pills, not yet!" bellowed Macdonald through the window.

Next door to the Globe Theatre was Garrett's store. Large display windows were set in a false front decorated with panels of crinkly-pressed sheet metal. John Garrett was a notable English cricketer before coming to mine on McKee Creek. Farther down was Pillman's small blue house, and his drugstore was another two houses down on the corner of Pearl and First. At the same corner stands the old Discovery jail house, built of six-by-six timbers. Iron bars cover its single cell window.

Across from the jail is Kershaw's hardware store. Kershaw came up the Telegraph Trail heading for Dawson City, but stopped over in Atlin and stayed to start a business. He made sheet metal goods, including stoves known as "Yukon Heaters," and sold skis and sporting goods. Every first of July, he put an ice-cream booth on the

The businesses along Pearl Avenue. *(Yukon Archives/Atlin Historical Society Collection, p.2350)*

boardwalk outside his store. He was one of the first people in Atlin to have a radio, and he often invited his neighbour Mrs. McIver over to listen to it. But she wasn't impressed; it wasn't like a gramophone and it didn't play her favourite hymn, "Nearer my God to Thee."

Jules Eggert's second store still stands on the corner of Pearl Avenue and First Street. This large barn-like building, with its pressed tin siding, was built soon after the 1916 fire. In front of this store, Eggert erected a clock as a gift to the citizens of Atlin. Decorated with ornate scroll work, the round clock rests on a classical Ionic column atop a cast-iron plinth. The clock was recently rebuilt and put in good working order by John Thoma, master welder, and Herman Peterson, genius with anything mechanical. Local artist Diane Smith painted the face.

The upstairs of this building is now used as a meeting hall for the freemasons. The Arctic Brotherhood, a type of Masonic fraternity, was conceived in February 1899 on board the *S.S. City of*

Seattle. Loaded with gold seekers, the ship was plying north to Skagway. The aim of the organization was "to encourage and promote social and intellectual intercourse and benevolence among men and to particularly advance the interests of its members and that of the North-West section of North America."

The brotherhood was open to any male of good moral character over the age of eighteen. The motto was "No Boundary Line Here," and the crest was a gold pan with a crossed pick and shovel superimposed and a Union Jack and the Stars and Stripes attached to the handle of each. Membership was granted only to those who lived north of latitude 54. The mother lodge in Skagway "promoted comradeship with the Alaskan and Yukon members of the Skagway Grand Camp to benefit northern miners and prospectors." Subsidiary camps were established in Atlin, Dawson City, and Nome, Alaska.

The Arctic Brotherhood held ritualistic ceremonies and had an elaborate hierarchy with a secret handshake, passwords, and regalia (a parka hood trimmed with white fur). The Grand Arctic Chief had a Recorder as secretary and a Keeper of the Nuggets as treasurer. Other officers were Arctic Chaplain, Camp Cook, Arctic Trail Guide, and Keeper of the Outer Tollgate. An Arctic Queen was referred to as Her Iciness.

The initiation ceremony for a "cheechako" — someone who had lived less than a year in the North — began with all participants repeating the rallying cry "Mush On" as the candidate entered. Then the Arctic Chaplain led the following invocation around an altar.

O, Jehovah ... supreme Director of the destinies of the Arctic Brotherhood ... I do solemnly promise, should I be able to endure the tests about to be applied, I will never reveal the grip, sign or password, or any of the secrets or mysteries of the Arctic Brotherhood ... I will never lead a brother Arctic on any false stampede, or make him false reports of new discoveries. I will always give a brother Arctic preference in buying, trading or employ-

*ing, everything else being equal. The latch string shall always be outside my
door to a brother Arctic, and with him I will share the comforts of life, and
give him shelter free, if for the time being he be short of funds. I will guard
and protect the virtue of all women and particularly those who may be re-
lated to an Arctic Brother by ties of blood or affection. I will never, in dis-
solving a partnership with a brother Arctic, cut a stove in two or split a tent.
I will never kick a dog, or work a horse with a sore spot on his back. To all
of which I pledge my honour.*

In the rough days of the gold rush, when law and order hung
by a thread, this was a measure of good faith and a model for
stampeders' behaviour. "The open hand of fellowship, aid when
overtaken by distress, and ready sympathy in time of sorrow," must
have given much comfort to young men suddenly launched into
an alien life in the Yukon wilderness far from the comforts of home.

The open ground below our cabin was the site of the Royal
Hotel — the starting point of the 1916 fire. The hotel was owned
by Louis Schulz, an entrepreneur commonly acclaimed "a prince
of a man." A large wood heater stood in the gambling room and
the chimney pipe went through the floor of the Schulz living room
above. The east wing was so cold it was known as "The Refrigera-
tor." During one cold snap, Lyme Hodge, a prospector who was
staying at the hotel, came down to the card room to warm up. He
lay down on a bench beside the barrel stove. A man came in from
outside with icicles hanging off his beard.

Hodge awoke suddenly, "My God, what's the number of your
room?" he asked.

In the Royal Hotel, Frank Henning, a practical joker, once
played a prank on Marco Pini, an Italian miner. While Marco was
sleeping off his booze, Frank nailed his shoes to the floor, hid in a
closet, and crumpled some newspaper loudly, shouting "Fire! Fire!"
Pini awoke hungover and confused, jumped into his shoes, and fell
flat on his face.

As well as owning the hotel, Louis Schultz ran a butcher's shop for Pat Burns, founder of a food business that still thrives in Whitehorse. He married Miss Daisy Durie of Tacoma, Washington, who, with her parents, climbed over the Chilkoot Trail and then turned east at Carcross to reach Atlin.

The meat trade was successful for several years, but eventually slowed down with the economic decline after the boom and bust of the gold rush. Burns gave the business, as a reward for years of service, to Schulz, who changed it to a general store.

Schulz and his partner formed a transport company and acquired the contract to carry the Royal Mail by horse-drawn stagecoach between Atlin and Carcross. They built several roadhouse shacks along the route for travellers to rest in. Sometimes, there were more bodies than beds, and people would bunk down in the barn or out in the open. One passenger, who slept under a tree at Moose Arm, was very much annoyed when he received a bill upon his arrival in Atlin: "$1.00 for bed."

Schulz grubstaked many prospectors, giving them money and food in return for a share in their mines. He loaned thousands of dollars he never saw again.

"Soup's on the table," he used to say. "Pay when you get the money."

When Schulz eventually became tired of people leaning on his generosity, he sent them to cut cord-wood that he would then buy back from them. He had aluminum coin-sized tokens with his name on one side and "Good for 25 (or 50) cents in trade" on the reverse.

"Miners would come into town with $200," he complained, "and instead of paying me the fifty they owed, they'd go to the liquor store. Then they'd come and ask me for credit."

With no road out of Atlin, there was little fear of his debtors absconding. But on one occasion, a man borrowed one of Schulz's rental bicycles to chase a fellow miner who, he claimed, owed him money and had taken off down the lake ice with it. The man on the bicycle caught up with his friend and they doubled each other to Whitehorse from where they returned the bike C.O.D.

Now we have reached the foot of Pearl Avenue and the natural harbour round which Atlin clusters. On the site of the old White Pass Hotel, which used to stand right here on the waterfront, Tom and Vera Kirkwood more recently built ten log cabins and ran a successful business renting them as self-contained units. Now they have retired and live in the renovated old Schulz residence on the lakeside.

Tom Kirkwood followed the mold of Atlin's many early businessmen. Soon after arriving in Atlin, he and two partners bought Engineer Mine for $5,000. Then he married Vera, who came to Atlin as the outpost nurse. Tom bought the hardware store, ran a taxi and the ambulance, edited the *Atlin News Miner,* started a broadcasting society that brought television to town, was secretary to the Board of Trade, and planned the reconstruction of the recreation centre and curling rink.

He was in the hot seat whenever a controversial enterprise arose in Atlin: the road link with the Alaska Highway, a plan to dam the Atlinto River to store water in the lake for the hydro dam in Whitehorse, the realignment of the airport, and a projected Mount Barnham molybdenum mine.

On the town block across from the Kirkwood Cottages stands the Atlin Inn. The windows of the bar of the Atlin Inn look out across the harbour to First Island. To the right, the *M. V. Tarahne,* now being restored, lies on ways. The inn was owned by Joe Florence until he was killed in an air crash at Dease Lake. He and his wife, Carol, drove up the Alaska Highway, noticed the sign for Atlin at Jake's Corner, and followed it to the end of the road — a common story.

They bought the run-down Atlin Inn and refurbished it. Carol ran the hotel and coffee shop, while Joe did maintenance and drove the sewage truck. He panelled the walls of the bar with wood from an old barn in Discovery. The weathered boards were rough and grainy, and water had stained them deep brown, grey, and silver. On the walls hung saws, axes, and machine parts that he had collected from mines and old cabins on the creeks.

Joe was a big man, both in build and personality; he wore size sixteen shoes. When talking to someone from behind the bar, he used to stoop slightly, as though trying not to appear head and shoulders above the person he was talking to in his soft southern drawl. Under short-cut hair, thick glasses stared out from a boyish face that readily broke into a smile.

His clothes fitted loosely, or not at all, and he moved with a gangly gait like Tom Sawyer returning home after a long day's fence-painting. Joe was a passionate fisherman, yet his hands were big as spades and seemingly unsuited to tying delicate flies. From his motorboat, he compiled a map of reefs that I used to supplement my own photographs taken when flying over the lake with Herman Peterson and Arden Hixson.

In such an isolated place as Atlin, it is easy to see why business has held such importance in people's lives. Indeed, despite road and air connections to Whitehorse and the outside world, it still does today.

✧✧✧

Old Timers

Before Gerry Andrews departed in the fall, along with the migrating geese and swans, he gave me a pile of ancient lumber that lay in his yard. I used it to face the walls and ceiling of the basement, and then I stacked heavy logs down there to fuel the furnace in the winter. I also built a box beside the basement door to hold kindling for the kitchen wood stove. Under snow, the outdoors woodpile keeps bone dry.

I walled the space around the furnace with asbestos sheets. This addition, along with the new chimney, made us feel secure in letting the fire roar each time we arrived in winter. Air, heated in the double skin around the barrel, rose through the open floor vents and warmed the sitting room and bedroom. The floor to ceiling aluminum stovepipe heated the kitchen. The cabin was now so well insulated that sometimes, when Sarah cooked on the wood stove, she had to open the front door to let in a blast of cold air.

Wood burning has its dangers. Chimneys need cleaning every couple of weeks, because wood smoke deposits creosote on the inside, especially if the fire is banked down to burn slowly. Cleaning the chimney involves climbing onto the roof and vigorously scrubbing the inside with a wire brush on a long pole. Burning the fire hot with a few logs at a time helps to minimize creosote deposit, but even then some of the creosote falls as red-hot soot into the sump at the elbow of the pipe (from which it can easily be removed).

When a chimney catches fire, it roars like a jet plane taking off on a clear cold windless day. It burns out all the accumulated creosote but generates tremendous heat within the chimney as it passes through the roof rafters, which can catch fire. The best firewood is spruce or pine cut where a fire has swept through the forest. Fire-killed wood that has had its bark scorched off loses much of its resin and makes less creosote than unpeeled wood.

One stovepipe fire had tragic consequences for old Jim Dawson, a patient of mine. Late one night, when the temperature had dipped below minus 40 degrees Celsius, he returned to his cabin after a visit to the pub in a village not far from Atlin. He lit the kindling and jiggled a hefty log through the furnace door. A final shove shifted the barrel-stove, and the stovepipe junction parted. Sparks shot out of the open end, and these ignited the tinder-dry 40-year-old roof timbers. Jim dashed for the door, stood panting in the freezing night air, and watched the bonfire that was once his home.

After the first paralyzing shock passed, Jim tried to salvage a few of his possessions from the blazing cabin. He tore down the door and was about to enter when flames licked some thirty-thirty shells stored on the windowsill beside his bed. They detonated and bullets whined about him like a machine-gun fusillade. Jim fled for his life and took cover behind a big standing pine tree. Snow on the cabin roof melted and ran down the walls. This dampened the flames slightly, but not enough to extinguish the blaze. Soon all that remained of the cabin was a charred heap of logs lying in a lake of melted snow. Jim's moose hide mukluks were soaked and he sank exhausted into a snow bank and slept soundly. While asleep, his feet froze.

On waking at first light, Jim crawled to the end of the lane. A passing truck took him into the village, and he was flown to Whitehorse. Both feet, at first a mottled, blistered purple colour, went gangrenous black from ankles to toes. With excellent nursing they remained free of infection, dried out over the next few weeks, and become like a pair of black leather ankle boots. Both feet had to be amputated below the knees in order to accommodate artificial legs.

Jim returned from rehabilitation in Vancouver some months later.

"Can't get 'em frostbit any more, can I, Doc?" he said to me as he knocked his new plastic legs with his sticks and danced a little jig to show off to the clinic nurses.

Sadly, that was not true, nor was it the end of the story. Two years later he got into the booze again. His propane ran dry, so, in his inebriated state, he climbed into a sleeping bag to stay warm. Eventually, having no more food, he struggled out to the road, but was unable to climb over the windrow pushed up by a road grader. He fell into a snow bank and froze his stumps, which caused him to have both legs amputated above the knees. Some years later I heard he had died — in a nice warm bed.

Our house, being opposite the grocery store, was a vantage point for the comings and goings of people at our end of town, especially of the old-timers Krist Johnsen and Russell Crowe. We often saw them shopping, but they rarely spoke to each other.

No one can remember the origin of their discord, and it is doubtful they knew it themselves. But each preferred to walk round the block rather than risk bumping into the other and having to pass the time of day — something they had not done for many years. When Krist went to the store, he always wore a dapper suit, polished brogue shoes, and a trilby hat. He had a hesitant, meticulously polite manner. He used to pick up a free copy of the *Atlin News Miner* from the store. Then he would go to Russell's cabin, hook the paper under the door knob, and walk away smartly.

"Goddamn Krist's been here," Russell would say on finding the paper, "but he wouldn't knock on the door. What's the matter with him?" Despite the outward hostilities, they spoke respectfully of one another and, deep down, were imbued with a mutual fondness.

We first met Russell Crowe, a Nova Scotian, rolling along the street on his way to the store. He moved like a schooner riding a heavy swell. You could always hear him coming because, being almost stone deaf, he shouted in a deep throaty roar at any passerby. He broadcast confidential conversations in a loudspeaker voice and issued tirades against the Indian villagers with whom he waged constant war. When we passed the time of day, he would fiddle with his proudly-worn hearing aid, which frequently emitted a high-pitched squeal.

Spectacles that looked like the bottoms of wine bottles balanced on Russell's bulbous nose. Snuff stained his nostril hairs brown, and strong nicotine irritated the red, rheumy lining of his nose. His shirt front showed a dusting of brown snuff, which he wiped away with the back of his weathered hands, toughened by a lifetime of mining. Like a hamster, he kept a wad of chewing tobacco pouched in his lower lip, and his teeth were blackened with thick black juice, a gob of which he occasionally spat onto the street.

Russell wore the same clothes day in and day out, whether to go fishing or to dance at the Moose Hall. His rotund belly protruded over sagging trousers, which were doubly supported by suspenders and a thick leather belt. Once a year he went to Whitehorse to buy a new outfit. He would return home with a bag holding the old clothes, which he then burned.

An avid fisherman, he owned a boat that he kept on the foreshore by Harper Reed's dock. During his winter hibernation, he read and tied delicate fishing flies with his horny hands. On light summer mornings he often rose at 3 a.m. and rowed or motored forty kilometres down the lake to Second Narrows. There, quite alone, he would camp and fish for several days.

Russell was born in Halifax County, Nova Scotia, in 1901 and was orphaned young. He lied about his age and joined the army

Russell Crowe (left) and Krist Johnsen (right). *(Yukon Archives/Atlin Historical Society Collection, pp. 2530, 2805)*

as a bugler boy at fifteen. He crossed the Atlantic on the *Olympic*, sister ship of the *Titanic*, and served in England for three years.

After returning to Canada, he came north and worked for a mining company in Atlin during the depression. He bought a lease on the lower end of Spruce Creek from an old miner. With gold at thirty dollars an ounce, he was soon making three times his company salary as well as employing three hired hands at seven dollars a day, board not included.

"I figured I might as well dig gold for myself instead of working for other people," said Russell. "It beat working for wages. I was getting whatever gold the old-timers left behind. I drifted underground, back upstream about 700 feet on a fifteen degree incline. When the old-timers mined, they left a lot of wooden props to hold the ground up. But we drove a tunnel way in across the pay streak, went to the back end, pulled out the pay dirt and let the roof cave in behind us. I found one 26-ounce nugget and several 10-ounce nuggets, as well as a lot of fine gold."

In the early days, if a miner found a little gold, he would build a house on his claim and stay there pushing his luck for the rest of his working days, even if the ground never produced much more gold. The claim below Russell's on Spruce Creek was known as

"The Boneyard" because men worked themselves to the bone look-ing for gold that wasn't there.

"I cleaned up the sluice boxes every Saturday afternoon. I'd say to the men: 'We'll see if we've been working this week by what's in the boxes.' When you're placer mining and you look in them boxes it just about hypnotizes you."

There were 800 miners in Atlin in the 1930s, many of them small operators like Russell. "She was a rip-snorting town in those days." he said. "Nobody went hungry, and you didn't know about the depression unless you turned on the radio."

Whenever we visited him in his cabin, he produced a torrent of stories about the rough characters of Atlin in the old days. A few people were killed in fights and one fellow was punched to death for fooling around with another man's woman. One day, an Atlin bully, drunk after a party, came to Russell's cabin.

"I can lick any so-and-so on Spruce Creek," the man bragged.

"Baloney, you couldn't lick nobody!" said Russell, who put a bear hug on the drunkard, threw him down, and held him there. "I'll let you up only if you're going to be a good boy," he said be-fore letting him go. Next day, the man apologized.

When Russell retired, he bought a cine camera, which he car-ried around town. He filmed everything that took his fancy. One day, I persuaded him to go sailing. For safety, I asked him to stand on the steps inside the cabin. He was busily shooting the town when the boat suddenly heeled in a gust of wind. He fell backwards onto the bunk cushions, while, pointing at the sky through the slid-ing hatch, the camera kept rolling. After this roll of film was de-veloped we met him in the street.

"I've had them filums back," he said, "and I wants you to come over and see 'em."

Sarah and I went to his cabin at the arranged time. The long, low house, once painted white with blue trim, stood across the street from the Merry's, close up against a line of poplar trees that obscured the lake. Three rooms led one into the other. All the windows were curtained, so the further in we went the darker it became.

In the tiny outside porch a gas stove stood on a counter beside an enamel basin full of unwashed dishes and heavy cutlery. A slop pail showed behind a curtain suspended on a springy wand below the dresser, and a half-full garbage bag lay in the opposite corner. He stored a small pile of split wood beside a tin Yukon stove, set in the middle of the floor.

"C'mon in while I gets the projector fixed," said Russell as he led us into a room illuminated with a single, bare, dim bulb. A large settee and a couple of metal and plastic dining chairs stood against the wall behind the table, where the projector was balanced on a pile of old *National Geographic* magazines. While he fiddled with the extension cord and adjusted the screen, we looked around the room. A string of coloured Christmas bulbs was plugged into the ceiling light fixture. Fishing tackle lay on the dresser, and spoons, lures, and flies were stuck into a curtain. Pages of a 1940 calendar that was tacked to the wall showed nubile maidens, naked except for a wisp of diaphanous silk draped across chest and crotch, sporting themselves on swings in the clouds.

"You'se best sit on the bed," Russell bellowed. A heavy khaki sleeping bag lay heaped on an iron bedstead in one corner of the room. The mattress was bare, the pillow had no case, and the still air was dankly ammoniacal, but Sarah and I did as we were told.

The movies were dismal, but Russell kept up a commentary on scene after scene of Atlin. The climax was a shot taken as he lay on his back, with the camera still whirring and pointing through the cabin hatch to the sky above. He offered us tea as an excuse to keep us a captive audience, willing though we were.

"I've been more or less a lone wolf ever since I got out of the army. I like it that way. If I wants to go some place, I just go. If you've only got the one suitcase, it's not hard on you, but when you've got a bunch of suitcases to move and maybe a bunch of kids too, you're really up against it. I never walked up the aisle, but I got no regrets neither. It don't stand to reason, this life after death," he continued philosophically as he poured us more tea. "You're just like a dishcloth: when it's wore out you throw it away. When I die, they'll take me up to the bone yard and put me six feet under-ground. There I am, dust to dust. Where we comes from and where we goes, nobody knows. I doubt I'll make it to meet Jerusalem Slim."

One day, Judith and I set out to visit Krist Johnsen. To reach his gate, we swung right onto Watson Street and cut diagonally across open ground below Aurora House. This one-time sporting house was built in 1901 by Carrie Walker. Several tiny rooms led off a short central corridor, like in a rabbit warren, and there was no sound-proofing in the walls. Business was once so brisk that an annexe had been added to the south side. Now, willow shoots grow through the floor of the porch, the windows are boarded up, and paint peels from the outside walls. But the bedrooms still have some remnants of the original luxurious purple and gold wallpaper.

Life in mining towns must have been lonely for bachelors. Entertainment in those days centred on the hotel bars and the sporting houses. "Sports," as certain ladies were called, were important in the social fabric of tough, raunchy mining towns like Atlin, where predominantly single miners were engaged in heavy physical labour. For a few minutes a week men could buy access to a sympathetic ear and intimacy denied them in the rough life on the creeks.

Sports got five dollars a shift and were moved by their madam to wherever their services were demanded along the road between Atlin and Discovery. They also sold booze and danced in hotels to the music of a Victrola — a sort of mechanical piano cranked with a handle.

The police constantly harassed Carrie Walker, and this caused her to write the following letter to 'The Hon. R. McBride, Premier of British Columbia:

Atlin B.C. Dec 21st. 1903

Dear Sir,

I have a grievance to lay before you — which I know you are in a position to rectify. I regret very much that I have to trouble you in this matter — but really I can not get any justice here from officials. My complaints are the following. I have been summons & I had to appear in Atlin on charges which I were not guilty — for instance giving Miss Ward liquor — I had to employ atty. — & was at expense of two days in Atlin. Charge was dismissed by the Judge — yet at the same time Chief of Police Mr. Owens arose in court & said it only means to bring her back or do it all over. My House has been closed every since & I am prevented from opening the same — as Heals orders are to arrest me when I do open House. Yet all other Sporting Houses are allowed to run & make all the noise they wish.

My House cost me two thousand dollars in Discovery & was the first to build in the lower end of town & then my place was supposed to be the dead line — which since they allowed two other House to go up & run beyond me between my place & the town. I never kept a noisy place. I can not account for it— except I do not attempt to bribe — which has been reported from some of the others.

Kindly give this your consideration — soon as convenient & with regrets at being compelled to lay my complaint before you.

Yours sincerely,
Carrie Walker

We do not know what the premier's response was to Miss Walker's letter, but she certainly continued as a successful businesswoman.

Another sporting house was located nearby on First Street — a little blue building with a corner bay window where the madam, Eva Daniels, sat in an alcove facing onto the street. She ran two houses, one in Atlin and one in Discovery, and travelled to and fro by buggy.

"You sure kept mighty busy some days," she said. "Especially when you had to take a shift at Halfway." Halfway House is situated beside the bridge where the Spruce Creek road crosses Pine Creek.

Some married men started taking an interest in two dark mulatto sports who worked at Halfway House. One day, when the girls went shopping in town, some of the miners' wives went up to their house in Discovery and broke their windows. The girls packed up and left town.

Eva Daniels eventually got married to an Englishman, settled down, and worked as a seamstress. She made flannelette kidney warmers, because many miners suffered from sore backs, lumbago, and sciatica. She also sewed moccasin booties for sled dogs. During her later years, she became eccentric and wore a man's hat punched in at the crown and a jacket made of duck and geese breast feathers given to her by an admirer. After her husband, Sammy, died, she never again slept in their bed, but used to sleep on the love seat in the front parlour. One night, she set fire to her mattress by smoking roll-your-owns in bed and died from severe burns.

Arriving at Krist Johnsen's back door, Judith and I knocked firmly; Krist is hard of hearing and sits in his front room with a radio blaring. After much sliding of bolts and locks, the door opened. He welcomed us into his sparsely-furnished and freshly-painted kitchen.

"Come in, come in," said Krist in his clipped, sing-song Scandinavian accent. He set about firing up his wood stove to boil water. "This is just a little shack. But Atlin's a lovely place. You just can't beat Atlin. I've been here nearly fifty years."

From his kitchen window, we could see several pieces of property he owned in that part of town, including three small shacks painted white with dark green trim, a bright orange shed, and a tall house that used to be a hotel and restaurant. For the past decade, a notice has been posted outside: "building and 5 beautyful lots for sale." But there have been no takers; the price is never quite right.

"I'm property rich, but dollar poor," Krist chuckled. "I take a long walk every day. In winter, I ski out the back of the house across the salt flats. That keeps me in shape."

We talked about Nordic skiing, a passion we share. He showed us an old pair of homemade hickory skis with loose leather bindings and pointed tips. Strips of hairy skin could be attached for climbing steep slopes. Fifty years before, he and some friends had built a ski jump north of town. They jumped off the Red Bluffs and landed well out on the lake ice — a spectacular feat considering their primitive skis.

He told us some of the stories of his long life. Born in 1902 to parents who were both from the north of Norway — his mother from Lofoten Island, his father from Narvik — he came to Canada in his early twenties. His uncle, who emigrated to Seattle and followed the Klondike gold rush north, suggested that Krist join him.

"I came to Whitehorse and stayed at the Regina Hotel," said Krist. "There a prospector told me, 'You should try Atlin. That's a nice little place.' So I did, and here I am still."

He bought a ticket to Atlin, hung around the town for a week, and then got a job at a mine on Ruby Creek. Later he worked at Engineer, Ruffner, and Noland Mines.

"We worked like slaves underground," he said. "It was tough, tough, tough. Wet all the time. Mud over the top of your boots. We lived four men to a small bunkhouse, and the smell was so bad you could cut it with a knife. Some guys never washed their underwear."

Krist developed tuberculosis, and the doctor said, "No more mining for you young man." So he quit mining and looked for another occupation.

He soon realized that more money could be made running a laundry and a shower house for miners, and it would be healthier than working underground. He bought a Maytag washing machine, a hand mangle, and some gasoline clothing irons, and hired a Scots laundress named Jennie Easdon.

Miners came in from the creeks on Saturday bringing their dirty clothes and bed linen to be washed. A hot water tank stood in the half basement off his kitchen, and Krist had constantly to keep the hot water pressure up for the showers and bathtub. The men had a thorough clean-up in the shower before dressing in clean clothes and going out for a night on the town.

"A dollar a shower was too cheap," he said. "It should have been two dollars. Some of the guys stood under the hot water for half an hour 'til they were played right out and couldn't take any more."

The mining companies on the creeks copied his idea and started their own wash houses. Despite the competition, Krist kept his laundry going for twenty-five years. From a little store beside his front gate, he also sold suits for Tip-Top Tailors, insurance for Great West Life, and various edibles.

He enjoyed telling tales about early Atlin residents.

"Swedes were a boozy lot," he said. "This man Conrad sent to Scandinavia for a wife — just like a mail order. A nineteen-year-old Finnish girl, Hanna, replied to his advertisement."

She sailed to Seattle via the Panama Canal and then boarded the coastal ferry to Skagway. From Skagway, she took the White Pass Railway, the paddle-wheeler *Tutshi*, the *Duchess* steam train, and the Atlin Lake boat *Tarahne*. It was a tiring three-week journey, especially for a girl who was anxious about meeting her blind-date husband-to-be.

"Conrad came into town to meet her. He was in the bar waiting for the steamer," said Krist. "He was damned drunk out of his skull, so by the time he reached the dock he was decked out goofy. His hat was askew and his pants fell down round his ankles. Every time he bent down to pull them up he fell over and had to start again. The poor girl was so disgusted she burst into tears. A local woman felt sorry for Hanna and took her in. She soon got a job on Ruby Creek as a camp cook. She married Gus Holmgren, another Swede, who also used to ski."

This sort of episode — or worse — must have been the fate of many a young girl lured to the gold fields by the prospect of untold riches, adventure, and a break from the dreariness of domestic life at home.

As we were leaving, Krist gave Judith a badge that he had won when he was competing as a young man back home. It was a tiny pair of skis hung from a ribbon of the Norwegian national colours.

We invited Krist for several Christmas dinners. After one such occasion, he wished to give Sarah a rocking chair to thank her. The chair was an antique that had been stored away for many years in one of his sheds. We looked out of the window and saw him turning onto Second Avenue. Then he saw Russell leaving his cabin. Not wanting to be seen carrying a chair through town, Krist made a detour around the block to approach our house from the opposite direction. That delicate chair now graces our living room where we can sit gently rocking and staring out of the window.

After a lifetime of working as a miner and serving miners, Krist retired to his cabin. "You just can't beat Atlin," he says repeatedly. "It's the most beautiful place in the world. Fresh air and clean water. I go back to the old country now and again, but I always return to Atlin."

Now, sixty seven years after his arrival, Krist is over ninety and has outlived Russell Crowe. He's still spry and youthful, a much loved and respected old-timer, and is a grandfather figure to our own children.

Life in Atlin in the early days was hard, but it bred many tough characters like Krist Johnsen and Russell Crowe. Sadly, that generation has now almost totally disappeared.

SPRING

The Spring Season

Spring is a cataclysmic event in the North. After six months of snowy winter, the days lengthen. As the sun rises higher in the sky, we begin to feel its warmth, and life suddenly wants to burst forth after hibernating for so long. Spring also signals the start of our more frequent visits to Atlin.

One fine spring day we set off down the Atlin Road. Every journey down the 100-kilometre road is an adventure. A breakdown in this wild, isolated country can be serious, especially in winter. The road starts at Jake's Corner — Mile 866 on the Alaska Highway, 80 kilometres south of Whitehorse, and about halfway from Dawson Creek in northern British Columbia to Fairbanks, Alaska. Beyond the defile of limestone cliffs that tower over Jake's Corner lie Teslin, Watson Lake, and destinations south.

The Alaska Highway was built in 1942 by 20,000 American soldiers, engineers, and Canadian civilians who used primitive equipment to push a road through sub-arctic forest. The route was meant to supply the army in the event that Japan invaded Alaska through the Aleutian Archipelago. The 2446-kilometre road took nine months to complete. Ironically, because of American censorship, Radio Japan was first to announce the meeting of American and Canadian construction crews. The Japanese congratulated and thanked them for finishing a project that would greatly assist their invasion of North America.

Jake's Corner is the namesake of Captain "Jake" Jacobsen, the commander of a U.S. Army Engineers camp that was once located in the area. On a bank below the gas pumps, rusting machinery — a road grader, a bulldozer, an International pickup, and bits and pieces of mechanical junk — stand as a testimonial to the construction of the Alaska Highway. Modern heavy maintenance equipment, which belongs to the Yukon Department of Highways, is parked at the end of the lot.

The Atlin Road follows the route originally surveyed in 1949. It was built in response to pressure by Atlin citizens for a link between Atlin and the Alaska Highway. The Canadian Army in Whitehorse oversaw the small construction crew that included surveyors and engineers, a crane operator, a bridge builder, and a rock blaster. Their orders, issued by top military brass, were to build a 100-kilometre-long wilderness road within five months and at least cost "over good ground with a minimum of cut and fill — to hell with good alignment." Surveyors learned the lay of the land from air photos. Then they sent a crewman ahead to climb a tree and flash a signal mirror for a compass bearing. The road, which wound between mountain buttresses and the lake shore, skirted ravines and muskeg. It was finished within the allotted time and budget. Many of the switch back curves and dips have since been ironed out, but it is still quite a challenging drive.

A short way from Jake's Corner is a junction: Atlin is to the left; Tagish and Carcross are straight on ahead. In winter, you can drive the Atlin Road without meeting a single vehicle. The summer differs; you may have to pass upwards of twenty tourists. Unused to serpentine roads, they roll up their windows against clouds of fine dust and, oblivious to honking horns, hug the crown of the road.

The dirt road is generally easier to drive in winter; the surface is graded smooth and cold dry snow gives traction to heavy-tread tires. Marker posts on the shoulder of the road indicate the depth of the snow. In summer, slippery loose gravel on the shoulders act like ball bearings, and red flags warn of potholes. Stones thrown up by oncoming vehicles cause cracks in windshields, which are a trademark of northern travel.

As we drive down the road, a large owl flies out of the trees near the lake and lazily flaps its wide-spanned wings. We climb a hill and slide over the far side. A carved wooden sign under a cliff tells of some mountain goats that were transferred to the area from Kluane Park. They have climbed over the mountain and sensibly stay out of the range of hunters' rifles. The road bank gives us a geology lesson. Below the topsoil of the berm lies a thin, chalky layer of White River pumice ash; a volcano in the St. Elias Mountains on the Alaska-Yukon border erupted 1,400 years ago and spread fine ash throughout the southern Yukon.

Large hoof prints in a snow ditch show where a moose crossed the road to the safety of the bush. When we first travelled the Atlin Road, we used to see at least one large animal — a moose, a caribou, or a bear — but over the years they have become scarce. Perhaps they are hunter-wise, or they may have been over-hunted. I imagine them watching us, camouflaged among the willows and ground alder by the roadside or peering out through branches of spruce and pine.

At the foot of Thirteen Mile Hill, a sign advises drivers without winter tires to put on chains. Near the top stands a box of sand for those who fail to reach the crest of the rim because of a spin-out on slick ice. The road passes through an area where a lightning-struck forest fire burned several years ago, scorching trees and laying them flat like jack-straws. Forest fires are a necessary part of the cycle of nature. They encourage the growth of willow shoots on which moose browse. Yukon forest fires are generally left to burn themselves out unless they threaten a community, roads, or vital land.

We pass a parked pickup. An Indian lad sits on the tailgate busily strapping on snowshoes. His grandmother scans the bush holding a rifle. Being aboriginal, they are not restricted to imposed hunting seasons. The road swings around a hill, and we see two golden eagles performing an aerial ballet — their courtship flight. They swoop and soar in long curving bow bends above their eyrie, high in a tree on the horizon. We have not seen them since.

Nearby, Tarfu Creek is backed up by a beaver dam. A one-room log cabin, a legacy of the survey crew who named this creek, stands above the bank. The name of the next creek south, Snafu Creek, is a military acronym that means "situation normal, all fouled up."

Cresting an esker, we look down on Atlin Lake. Abeam on our right is tent-shaped Mount Minto. Its Tlingit name, Kee-yun, means "the only mountain where hemlock grows at its feet."

Suddenly a gargantuan fuel truck barrels towards us and forces us onto the shoulder. Loose shoulder gravel plays hell with the steering, and the experience leaves me tingling — my stomach an empty pit. At the Yukon-British Columbia border, a plethora of road signs is an unwelcome brush with civilization. In the Yukon, we are told, distance is now measured in kilometres, headlights are required by law at all times, radar detectors are illegal, and the territory is a nuclear-free zone . . . but please come back soon to the Magic and the Mystery of the Land of the Midnight Sun. Signs on the other side of the road inform us that the use of seat belts is compulsory in British Columbia, export permits are required by hunters, and livestock is prohibited on highways. This last bit of information is conveyed by a diagonal red line across a horse that looks as if it has been struck by a thunderbolt.

A red flag in the ditch warns of a creek that has overflowed, forming a dirty, rust-coloured "glacier" that spans the road. Nearby is a house-sized boulder, a glacial erratic, which may have dropped off the edge of a retreating glacier aeons ago when this area was a glacial lake. Alternatively, the boulder may have been stuck in a huge iceberg that later melted.

Hitchcock Creek, where the road runs close by the lake, is the step-off point for crossing to the foot of Mount Minto. There we pass an orange survival shelter — a refuge for stranded travellers. A deep dip ahead brings forth spine-chilling memories. There, I once spun two 360s after touching my brakes on some ice while driving too fast. Very shaken, I ended up pointing in the direction I was bound. At the top of the next hill one Christmas, Sarah slid off the road and landed softly in a snow ditch. Near Trudeau's sawmill, on an early summer morning, we once saw a full-curled Dall ram, a mother sheep, and some kids licking salt off the road.

The scenery, a gaunt wilderness of a zillion conifers, abundant lakes, and rough rock, seems content in its desolation. After Base Camp Creek, pine and spruce give way to aspen and birch. The low sun casts tree shadows across the road. At Indian River Ranch, a bountiful crop of hay grows where scrubby bush has been cleared to make open fields. Outfitters' horses are corralled by criss-cross poles of lodge pole pine and zigzag fences. In winter, swags of snow lying between these logs make patterns in the bland whiteness.

At Davie Hall Lake, the road has been surveyed for widening and the bush trimmed. Horses from Goodwin's Farm forage the ditches of Fourth of July Creek. Several float planes are beached at Como Lake, where children swim in summer. This spot is usually a placid haven for landing planes when stormy weather causes the wind to screech down Atlin Lake. A bald eagle scares scavenging ravens away from the garbage dump that lies in a kettle depression near the road.

A panorama of mountains suddenly bursts upon us as we approach Atlin. Road banks are mucky where slushy snow is mixed with the sand and gravel put down by maintenance crews. As the snow melts, garbage surfaces in the ditches, and pools of murky water collect in culverts only to freeze again when night brings colder temperatures.

In town, thawing rays of sun cause snow to avalanche off the roofs of the cabin and the biffy. The children stomp through the thin layer of morning ice formed over pothole puddles. They are excited to be in Atlin again after the long winter, and spring brings us all a sense of renewal and the anticipation of many adventures in the coming summer.

As we sit on the deck and drink our morning coffee, we enjoy the spectacle of returning flocks of snow buntings. Swirling in scintillating clouds, the white feathers on the undersides of their wings a contrast to their black backs, they swoop and settle in a patch of snow for a few seconds and then take to the air again. Legions of little grey birds of no distinguishable species harbinger lengthening days ahead, when green grass will replace snow. Hummingbirds sometimes stray inland riding favourable winds northward on their spring flight up the coast of Alaska. A friend of mine, while climbing in the St. Elias Range on the south side of Mount Logan, Canada's highest peak, found a hummingbird at 5,000 metres. To this day, the spot is known as the Hummingbird Ridge.

Soon, flocks of swans and geese, their necks outstretched and their powerful wings beating noisily, will fly over the house in loose V-formation. They will be heading towards their breeding grounds in the boreal forest and tundra of the northern Yukon and Alaska. There may be 300 birds in a single flock, and with a strong tail wind, they can fly at 80 kilometres per hour. They rest in the slough between Krist Johnsen's place and the Indian village, also a sanctuary for ducks and marsh waders.

In spring several hundred tundra and trumpeter swans, Canada geese, and assorted ducks, waterfowl, and gulls gather holus-bolus in lakes to rest and feed in preparation for their long journey north. Tundra swans make a high-pitched whistling; trumpeters honk loudly. Their number swells tenfold in the ensuing hectic weeks. In shallow water, they bob, tails-up feeding on plant roots. Some stand on the ice shelf in the cool of evening, a time when many birds become active and excitable.

Without warning, a flock takes off, flies a circuit in formation, and returns, feet extended, wings at full flap, and flaring before touchdown, to settle on the water. Another flock, white birds shimmering against a dark background of spruce, continues northward. Swans and geese need every minute of the short Arctic summer to hatch their eggs and nurture their chicks so that their offspring will be big enough to fly south in the fall. Myths abound over the signal which announces to the birds that water is open further north. Do scouts go ahead and return to tell the flock? Does lengthening daylight trigger the urge to move on? Usually, families stay together on the long migration south, but sometimes an early freeze-up in the tundra induces adult swans to fly off and leave their young to perish.

Once past the vernal equinox, the evenings lengthen, days become warm, and pussy willows hang on the branches. But snow remains on north-facing mountainsides and covers still-frozen lakes. In the bush and on open eskers, snow melts as the sun strengthens. Travellers returning from Vancouver and Victoria tell of daffodils in bloom, cherry blossoms, and green grass — the stuff that dreams are made of. As soon as the snow disappears from sun-bathed banks beside the Atlin Road the first spring crocus, Pulsatilla (truly an anemone), bursts out of the shriveled skeletons that were last year's growth. Its cup-shaped purple bloom has bright yellow stamens set around a central purple eye. After snow has blanketed the land for half a year, it is difficult to imagine how these plants have ever survived. That they bloom again is an annual miracle.

As spring unfolds, the hills become piebald, but gullies on the north side of Monarch Mountain are still full of snow. The sun roams across the sky, and the western face of the mountain stands out in contrast to the rest of its shadowed mass. Poplar trees have a faint sheen before the shiny, sticky outer coat of their buds breaks like a chrysalis unfolding. Next, aspens and willows start to leaf. The tender green of the first buds lasts only a couple of weeks, and then leaves turn dark green and meld with the pine and spruce forest.

Northern harriers patrol the ditches and swoop on mice and gophers, while ravens caw "quork, quork" from telegraph poles.

Small animals emerge after hibernating in burrows. Some have
passed a more active winter and have roamed freely in the air pocket
between the base of the snow pack and the frozen earth. Every
seven to ten years, the population of the predominant species crashes
and another takes its place. Squirrels dance across the ski trails chat-
tering excitedly, and race through tree branches as they defy grav-
ity. The ruff around the ankles of snowshoe hares supports them on
top of the snow crust and makes a spoor much larger than their foot.
Arctic ground squirrels, commonly known as gophers, stand on
their haunches at the roadside and scuttle off into burrows. After a
tranquil winter, they are unused to rolling wheels, and many become furry pancakes on the road.

After noon great mushroom clouds of cumulus build, wild local thunderstorms darken quadrants of the sky, and short sharp
showers empty the clouds of their moisture. All the while, the horizon is bathed in sunshine. On chilly spring nights, the aurora
borealis (or Northern Lights), appear as moving curtains of light,
often sweeping across the sky. Caused by electrically-charged ions
in the upper atmosphere, they are coloured pink if the ions are of
oxygen and green if they are of nitrogen. I once saw the Atlin sky
a rare vermilion; lights exploded from a focal point overhead like
red fireworks.

Frost persists on clear April nights. Sarah's green fingers awaken
when the beds start to unfreeze, and she digs the recently frozen
soil as soon as it is soft enough to turn. But the compost heap, still
in shadow, shows shiny shards of ice like permafrost. She plants
California poppy and delphinium seeds around the woodpile to
make a wild garden, and in the potato patch I grow Yukon Golds
and Atlin Reds. A Prince Edward Islander advised me to add a
sprinkle of sulfur to the soil for extra acidity and to mix seven parts
local clay to three of peat and two of sand, and a Saskatchewan

farmer told me to water them only sparingly; I follow the advice of both.

Spring can be dangerous for lake travellers who have grown complacent in using the hard-frozen ice. This is break-up season when ice metamorphoses and the melting snow forms surface water that percolates between the planes of hexagonal crystals. Eventually, the whole thickness of ice becomes honeycombed with vertical "candles" — like millions of ice pencils standing on end with nothing to bind them. With a tinkling sound, the candles collapse like dominoes and deep rumblings indicate the cracking of huge plates of ice. After a cold winter, the surface ice may be three metres thick; in a mild year it measures less than a metre. If the big lakes break up and go out early, giant slabs of ice careen down the rivers and form massive ice jams. When water backs up behind them, these dams can suddenly burst and flood land downstream.

One sparkling May morning shortly before break-up Wayne Merry had an icy experience. He set off to ski across Atlin Lake with a friend Stefan, and Stefan's dog, Butch. Wayne tested the ice through a crack near the shore in front of the Atlin Inn and found thirty centimetres of clear, hard ice. They skied on frosty snow between glassy patches towards the mouth of Torres Channel, keeping well apart to spread their weight. Near river outlets the ice is always dangerous, since the current constantly erodes it from below. Fifty metres from shore Stefan, who was in the lead, broke slowly through mushy ice and sank to his waist, struggling wildly.

Wayne, aware of the danger of rescuer turning victim, moved cautiously towards him. While sticking his ski pole into the ice, it suddenly gave way under his skis and he sank, gasping with cold, through the slush of rotten candles. He thrust his hands down into the numbing water and released his ski bindings. Remembering that in spring trappers often carry a long spruce pole to bridge the ice in case they break through, he brought his skis to the surface with hopes of using them to lever himself out of the water.

Several times, Wayne gently eased his waist out, but the ice around him broke and he slithered back into the water. Sodden clothing had doubled his weight, and his hands were so numb that he couldn't release the waist belt of his waterlogged pack. He began to lose strength and hope and coolly decided his time was up. He summoned all his energy for a final escape attempt and started thrashing towards the shore, clawing through the candled ice with his forearms. Stefan followed suit.

They both kicked bottom simultaneously and let out feeble cries of relief. Staggering out of the water and stumbling to the forest edge, they scraped together some dry leaves and pine twigs. With difficulty they lit a match and started a fire well away from the trees. Wayne remembered Jack London's story about a man lighting a fire under a tree with his last match and how the snow had melted and avalanched off the branches to extinguish the flames — and his chances of survival.

Shivering uncontrollably with hypothermia, they staggered about the beach to collect firewood. Their legs cramped as their limbs started to thaw. The pain was at first pricking and then excruciating, burning, gnawing. Glad to be alive, they warmed themselves thoroughly and dried their clothes by a roaring fire.

They walked along the shore to a point where the ice was usually thick and set off to ski home on a firm surface. Suddenly, they hit a patch of slush. The dog broke through and Wayne, who dared not go too close to the rotten edge of the ice, threw a noose of rope to the pleading dog and encouraged him to climb out onto the ice. Butch let out a despairing howl, followed by a single, clear, plaintive bark. Silence followed. Stefan and Wayne returned to shore where they found an abandoned cabin to camp in. In the morning, a helicopter responded to their signal flares, and their brush with hypothermia was brought to an end.

In spring, not only do the swans and geese return from wintering in the south, but so also come the gold miners. They crank up their machinery again and start digging as soon as the frost seeps out of the ground and the creeks begin to run. Because it is clear that gold created the town of Atlin nearly a century ago, the reader might suppose that the golden era came to a close soon after. Not so. Mines still flourish and vary in size from one-person, pick-and-shovel operations to large company endeavors backed by heavy-duty equipment and investment. As the gold market fluctuates so do the fortunes of the miners, big or small, and this reflects on the economic health of Atlin, which has little other than its scenic beauty to generate dollars.

John Harvey used to mine on McKee Creek, fifteen kilometres south of Atlin. When Sarah, the children, and I first visited him, we walked up a track leading off the Warm Bay Road and crossed a small creek overgrown with willow and alder. Beyond was a surreal landscape of jumbled boulders and rocks strewn topsy-turvy like upheavals from a violent earthquake. Nearly a hundred years of placer mining has scraped the valley floor bare of vegetation and has left a residue of rock and gravel (or tailings). Placer-gold deposits lie in the sand, gravel, and earth of stream beds or in alluvial debris eroded in ages past from the mother lode hidden somewhere deep in the earth. The detritus of the placer-mining operation on McKee Creek spewed out of the sluice boxes and formed hillocks, channels, potholes, and winding creek beds. Prospectors' discarded claim stakes, mighty timbers, and lengths of wide-bore rusty pipe were scattered at random among the rocks. The mine, situated high up the creek, faced the south end of Atlin Lake.

We arrived to find John Harvey seated outside his shack panning for gold. His weather-beaten face was framed by a jet black beard, his hairy forearms were suntanned, and his fingers were gnarled from manual labour.

"Hi! grab a pan and pull up a stool," said John. "This tub has last week's clean-up in it."

Beside him lay a chipped enamel washtub full of dirty water and gravel. He used a pie-shaped gold pan to scoop up some mud and then he swirled it in a smooth circular movement. Angling the pan forward slightly and using a centrifugal motion, he washed away the dirt until a thin crescent of heavy, ore-bearing black sand remained in the bottom. Eventually small flakes of gold sparkled against the black sand like a comet's tail. He washed away the sand until only gold flakes or, if he was lucky, a nugget was left behind.

"Why don't you guys have a try?" he said. "I'm off to the sluice box. Pan as long as you like, and then come up and join me."

As we panned, the children became fascinated by the notion that the tub was full of the sludge of tons of earth that had been washed through John's sluice box. The gold pans we held were the final stage of that entire mining operation.

After an hour, we walked up the hill above the sluice box to a pond where John was working.

"I've dammed the creek here," he said. "It's only a trickle in summer. But quite a head of pressure builds up when the water's piped down to the monitor."

Sections of wide metal pipe led from a control gate in the dam wall. The pipe fed water a kilometre downhill into the monitor, which was a cast-iron water cannon with a metal handle secured amidships and counterbalanced by a wooden box full of stones. By swivelling the monitor on a ball-and-socket joint, John pointed its barrel up, down, and sideways. He turned on a large valve and the trickle of water spilling from the nozzle became a powerful jet that arched across the valley. By aiming the water at the base of one wall of the creek, John undercut some of the exposed conglomerate rubble. It broke away and was washed down as a dirty stream of mud, gravel, and rolling stones into the catchment area where we stood. With a Caterpillar bulldozer, John pushed the gold-bearing pay dirt towards the wings of the sluice box that lay below us. To avoid clogging the sluice, he used a front end bucket to scoop waste rocks out of the murky stream.

This type of mining, known as hydraulic mining, was always popular on McKee Creek, which produced only a sixth the gold of Pine Creek. The cost of extracting the gold was high, and small operators quickly sold out to big companies that used steam shovels and hydraulic machinery. In the early days, the Atlin Mining Company and the McKee Consolidated Company joined forces to form the Amalgamated McKee Mining Company. This company combined with McKee Consolidated Hydraulic Ltd. to form the Pittsburgh-British Gold Company Ltd.

Several years after our visit with John Harvey, our son Adam spent a couple of summers learning the elements of gold mining by operating the monitor on a placer mine at Hunker Creek in the Klondike. Here, Mike Stutter and his partner drill core samples to estimate how much gold to expect from each cubic metre of dirt. Over a number of years, they have shaved the top off a hill on their mining property with front-end loaders, earth-moving scrapers, and dump-trucks. Some mining outfits in Atlin have used similar techniques on the tailings of Pine Creek, although now that ground is nearly played out.

We walked down to the sluice box, a wooden frame a metre wide and 20 metres long, which has coconut matting laid in the bottom. Flanged wings direct the stream into the box. Riffles, made of angle-iron bars pointing downstream, are set across the box so that the water flowing over them eddies back on itself. Heavy gold particles fall through the riffles and are caught on the matting. Larger nuggets that roll past are caught in the nugget trap, a metal frame in the shape of a Union Jack set half-way down the length of the box. Muddy water pours out of the end of the box into a settling pond that protects water-life downstream from being polluted — as required by mining laws.

Scattered at random over the tailings around John Harvey's mine, we noticed sections of metal pipe that were marked "L.P." — the initials of the former owner. Louis Piccolo came to Atlin in 1932 to work for Marco Pini, a fellow Italian. Louis and his brother lived in Pini's bunkhouse on Spruce Creek and ran a sporting house in Discovery — a dollar a drink and five dollars a girl.

Louis Piccolo started hydraulic mining on McKee Creek under foreman George Adams. They used dynamite to loosen the banks of the valley edge and monitors to wash the dirt down into the stream bed. Using these techniques, Piccolo could move 1,000 cubic metres of gravel in six hours. Soon he went off on his own and mined the ground for the next thirty-five years. Adams, sadly, was killed when he was thrown against a rock face by the jet of a monitor.

"I've got gold fever. Christ, I have it," Louis once said. "It gets into your blood so you can't quit. Sometimes you make a good clean up; next time bum. But it's always next time, next time. You work like a bugger, but you're happy. You spend money on drink and poker, but you're always optimistic. All miners die broke."

As I watched John Harvey rake the riffles, I thought that he shared some of the same philosophy towards gold as Piccolo.

"I clean up about once a week," said John. "First the riffles have to be removed, then I wash the coconut matting. At the end of the season, I burn the mats and pan the ash in case any gold flakes remain trapped in it."

In 1981, John and his partner, Harvey Evenden, found a 3 lb. 9 oz. (36.88 troy ounce) gold nugget halfway down their sluice box. Only fate saved that nugget. The size of a cigarette pack, it was too large to fall between the riffles and was nearly washed out of the sluice box along with the waste rock tailings. The two miners spotted it lying in the box. They picked it up and immediately stopped work and went off to celebrate and show off their prize at the Atlin Inn.

As we walked back to John's cabin, sunlight sparkled on the azure lake in the distance. All around us, McKee Creek was a devastated area that would stir the bile of any conservationist. But that scar is similar, in some respects, to a farm where men have transformed the landscape by stripping out trees to fence, ditch, and plant. From the air, the gold-mining scar is small compared to the vast area of surrounding wilderness. When mining ceases on McKee

Japanese miners from McKee Creek are lined up to leave town.
(Yukon Archives/Atlin Historical Society Collection, p.928)

Creek, willow scrub and alder will grow quickly over the tailings that bear witness to the labour that helped open up this country and, ultimately, allowed us to enjoy it.

McKee Creek was the scene of a strange incident in 1902. The manager of an hydraulic company, claiming that white men worked only long enough to acquire a grubstake, brought in 150 Japanese labourers to work his mine at considerably lower than the going wage. Local miners held a mass protest meeting in Atlin, where they openly stated that they wished to keep Atlin a white man's camp — no excuses given for racism. They sent a delegation to the Gold Commissioner, but he was absent. His deputy, Ned Thain, the Mining Recorder, was somewhat nervous about the brewing storm.

Next morning, the miners lined up on Pearl Avenue and marched off towards McKee Creek, 24 kilometres distant. Knowing the Japanese were armed with rifles, Thain feared bloodshed. So he recruited a teenage Guy Lawrence (of Yukon Telegraph fame), swore him in as special constable, and gave him a badge of office. Thain stood beside the trail as the miners left town and read the "Riot Act" to each man as he passed. Constables Walter Owen and Billy Vickers hastily drove a dog sled ahead to warn the McKee Creek mine manager of impending trouble. By evening, the miners reached McKee Creek where the armed Japanese were herded into a large log house. A tense showdown was defused by the constables, who escorted the Japanese back to town and put them on the stagecoach to Carcross.

Within a year, Constables Vickers and Owen were busy again on McKee Creek when the sluice boxes of the Hydraulic Company were robbed in the middle of the night. The company was using two large monitors to sluice the richest part of its claim. On this occasion, electric lights that enabled miners to work round the clock went out around midnight. The night watchman reported the blackout to the mine manager, who put off doing anything about it until morning. The shift foreman noticed that several riffles had been carefully removed from the last sluice box and the side wall had been sawn out. They found several ounces of coarse gold in the creek bed nearby, along with a saw, some tools, and gunny sacks.

The police watched Atlin's few possible exits. They rounded up some unsavory characters from the bars in Discovery and locked them in the jail house in Atlin, but they couldn't nail any of them. To this day, no one knows who the robbers were, nor the value of the stolen gold. But it was a lot.

One summer day, our family visited an old dredge that stands on Blue Canyon above Spruce Creek. This dredge is smaller than, but similar to, those that worked on McKee Creek in the 1920s. We climbed all over the structure to find out how it works. We discovered that a dredge is like a huge house built on a barge that floats in a shallow pool formed behind a dam on a creek. Using a belt of buckets that circulates continually, it scoops up dirt like a dinosaur grazing. The dirt is lifted high into the dredge housing and is tipped onto sluice boxes arranged in stacks, like a stairway with many landings. Water pumped up from the pond washes the dirt and digests its gold. The dirt is deposited on another belt in a huge arm that projects from the stern of the dredge. The dredge pivots on a lynch pin driven into the ground and spews the detritus out in the form of tailings. By swinging in an arc, the dredge remakes the downstream wall of the pond in which it floats. From the air, the old tailings make a semicircular pattern that looks like gigantic earthworm casts.

Placer gold mining operations all follow the same common path that ends in the gold pan, be it with pick and shovel, bulldozer and monitor, or dredge. The essence is to wash gold bearing dirt, preferably tons of it, through a sluice box to collect the concentrate and to pan it until the gold shines through the black sand. For nearly a century, people have mined McKee Creek. Very few have won big stakes; most have lost money and have seen their dreams shattered. Like gambling, mining is compulsive and addictive. It hooks the likes of John Harvey, who gave up a comfortable job in advertising in Toronto to shift mountains of dirt through his sluice box in hopes of finding the gold nuggets that would make his fortune.

As spring progresses, bets are placed at the Atlin Inn on when a barrel, placed between the town and First Island, will plunge to the bottom. It is weird to think that we will soon be sailing on water where so recently we skimmed the surface on skis, oblivious to reefs and the abyss below.

Spring seems to pass in the blink of an eye, and we are then hurtled into summer. The days are so long that you can read a newspaper outdoors at midnight, mosquitoes drone when the air is still, it's hard to get children to bed, and people are out and about until all hours doing activities they could only dream about in the dark of winter.

Tlingits

Looking left from the cabin, you can see the southern point of the bay in front of Atlin. There, with about twenty houses clustered near it, stands a white church with a cross atop the tower. This is the Indian village where several families of Taku River Tlingits live.

Jennie Jack held a traditional Tlingit wedding one summer on the open grassy point of Five Mile Bay, south of Atlin. Sarah and I were invited, having known the Jacks since we first arrived in Atlin.

Antonia, daughter of Chief Taku Jack, had seven children. Jennie is the youngest and has fire in her belly. Active in Indian politics since her teens, she was on the Atlin band's committee to negotiate aboriginal land claims. Two summers after enrolling at the University of British Columbia to study law, she and her niece Lucille went to Oka, Quebec to support the Mohawk struggle against the local council (whose members were intent on building a golf course on an ancient Indian cemetery). Jennie was seen on national television as she defused a confrontation between a soldier and a Mohawk warrior. Along with the Mohawks, she took refuge in the treatment centre at Oka and negotiated for peace with the Quebec police. She and others were charged with inciting mischief, but the case, which threatened her law career, was quashed.

Each of the Jacks is outstanding in different ways. The eldest brother, Sylvester, was band chief for several years and now runs a commercial fishing enterprise on the Taku River. He is assisted by Edward who in his youth drank methylated spirits that crippled and blinded him. Nevertheless, he reads widely through talking books and maintains the outboard engine on his boat, in which he goes fishing alone. Kaushee helped start the women's movement in Whitehorse, where the women's shelter was posthumously named after her. Josephine was sent away to residential school and later completed her education on her own. Then there is Tom, a helicopter pilot and professional guitarist; and George, who runs his own electrical contracting business and is an accomplished sailor.

To reach the site of Jennie's wedding, Sarah and I sailed down to Five Mile Point on a stormy day. Rain fell before we reached the broad beach where we had moored the year before to listen to a folk music festival. We tied up alongside George's trimaran, *Wild Onion.* Our orange sailing suits matched the colourful clothing of the elders, who wore traditional scarlet blankets adorned with buttons.

The kinship patterns of the Tlingit are complex. Their matrilineal society is divided into Wolf and Crow (Raven) clans whose membership used to be basic to a person's social life. Essentially "mother's people" are those of one's own clan, while "father's people" are the other half of one's social world. Both halves of the clan are needed to make a whole. One needs father's people to help one through the crises of everyday living — being born, growing up, marrying, and dying. Thereby, no one lacks for support and help in time of material need or spiritual crisis. This mutual and reciprocal daily give-and-take is fundamental to a strong family system, and determines who may marry whom.

A Crow must marry a Wolf and vice-versa. In the past, people who married within the clan were considered incestuous and so were barred from ceremonial potlatches. Some were even put to

death. One elder recounts how when she was at school it was un-
seemly for two Crows or two Wolves to talk and laugh together:

"Crow, when he made people, he made a Crow woman and
he made a Crow man too. And he made them marry each other.
And they were shy to each other and wouldn't talk to each other.
So Crow changes partners and, by gosh, they start to laugh and play
with each other and they're not shy any more."

At Jennie's wedding, the elders were seated on logs facing each
other, Crows opposite Wolves. They were surrounded by an altar
of spruce boughs, and a fire burned in the middle. On the Crow
side were Sylvester, then chief of the Taku River Tlingits; Frank
Jackson, leader of the Teslin Tlingit clan; and Antonia, Jennie's
mother. On the Wolf side were Helen Carlick and Elizabeth
Nyman, who had adopted the bridegroom, a white man, into the
clan at a smoking party a week before.

The bride, wrapped in a yellow blanket, was guided by her sister
to a "hiding place" behind a button blanket tied between two trees
30 metres away from the fire pit. From there, a carpet of animal
skins, beaver alternating with otter, was laid on a path leading to
the altar.

First, Elizabeth Nyman spoke to Antonia Jack: "My brother has
been waiting for your daughter a long time. When she goes away
on business, he gets lonesome for her, so we give him the name
Crying Wolf. We ask permission for your daughter to marry my
brother."

"I know Crying Wolf long enough that I'm not afraid to let my
daughter go to be his wife," replied Antonia.

Then she beat a drum and called to the bride to come out from
her hiding place. The bride, clothed in a decorated deerskin dress,
appeared from her hiding place and walked slowly, head bowed,
towards the fire. "Take your time, don't walk too fast," sang Antonia.
"It's sometimes difficult where you go, so take it easy. Go really
slow."

The bridegroom stood to receive his bride, and they sat beside each other on the Wolf log. He was then questioned by the elders about his sincerity in entering into the marriage. The couple gave each other rings and the elders exchanged gifts — vests, moccasins, and other pieces of clothing. Many of those present then performed a drum dance. Meanwhile, rain lashed down on the wedding party and Birch Mountain, in the background, was wreathed in cloud as the ceremony drew to a close.

Atlin Indians are an inland branch of the coastal Tlingit. The coastal Tlingit subsisted on a cornucopia of food from the sea: salmon, sea otters, and seals. Massive cedar trees in the rainforests provided timber for building and bark for weaving clothing and baskets. Their ancestral home is Angoon, a town on the west coast of Admiralty Island off the mouth of the Taku River and near present-day Juneau, Alaska.

The inland Tlingit have traditionally inhabited the land drained by the Yukon River. This dry plateau is frozen in winter and is covered with a spindly boreal forest, where hunting for food — caribou, moose, small game and birds — is arduous. The inland Tlingit entered the interior through breaches in the rugged mountain range that sweeps down the coast from southern Alaska into the Panhandle. A relief map of the coast shows the strange geography of glaciated mountains that are breached by the Chilkoot and White Passes towards Carcross and by the Taku River towards Atlin. Taku is an abbreviation for Tah-wakh-tha-ku, which means "the place where the geese sit down." Indian legend tells how the glacier Kadischle, now called the Norris Glacier, surged right across the mouth of the Taku River, damming it and forming a lake where geese and ducks rested on their northern migration. In the mid-eighteenth century, the Norris Glacier supposedly coalesced with the much larger Taku and Hole-in-the-Wall Glaciers that arise from the same névé but flow and behave differently. The snouts of these glaciers are the main obstruction to building an often-proposed road down the west side of Taku Inlet to join Juneau to Atlin.

Legends speak of Indian hunters around Taku who noticed that the glacier spewed out man-made artifacts, like baskets or broken arrows, which drifted across the lake and beached on the shore. These objects suggested that other humans lived nearby. Some Indians set off to investigate, and the chief gave them a magical iron hatchet as a parting gift. On their journey, the Indians saw smoke. Then some Atlin Indians appeared and spoke a strange language. The Taku Indians cut down some trees with the magical axe and made piles of wood. This impressed the newcomers, who had no such tools. The Atlin Indians gave gifts of furs to the Taku Indians who, in turn, gave them the magical axe. Thus began trade between the coastal and the inland people.

The coastal Tlingit would take advantage of south-westerly summer winds to sail up Taku Inlet into the Taku River, which is wide and tortuous. It could also be perilous because of big hidden rocks, massive log jams and sweepers, sandbars, and beaver dams. In large dugout canoes they raised square loose-footed sails on a yard-arm, one sail on either side of the mast. Thus they ran before the wind and against the strong river currents. They had to be wary of gales that blew in off the Pacific Ocean, which built up six-metre tides at the mouth of Taku Inlet.

The Taku River is navigable up to Tulsequah for large flat-bottomed boats. Thereafter, only canoes can follow the braided streams to the junction of the Inklin and Nakina Rivers. The gateway to the Atlin region is the headwaters of the tumbling Nakina and Sloko Rivers. The inland journey to reach Atlin follows an old Indian trail that traverses up and down deep ravines, through dense spruce and pine forest, and across swampy valleys full of buck brush. Through this country, the Silver Salmon Creek leads to Kuthai Lake, which flows into the O'Donnel River, which eventually finds its way into the south end of Atlin Lake.

This interior country became home to three Tlingit-speaking bands: Tagish, Atlin and Teslin. Why these people left the coast for the rigours of the interior is not clear. All interior Indians are considered as foreigners or *gunana* by the coastal Tlingit, despite the fact that the interior Tlingit speak a tongue similar to that of their ancestors in Angoon.

Historically, cultural traditions like Jennie Jack's wedding were ill-understood by white people. This was particularly so in the residential schools where children were sent to be de-Indianized and converted to Christianity by Catholics or Anglicans. Catholics from Beaver Creek on the western Yukon-Alaska border were sent 1,000 kilometres to attend boarding school at Lower Post near Watson Lake; Protestants were gathered from all over the territory to attend school in Carcross. At the age of five, Jennie Jack's sister Josephine was sent to residential school at Lejac (near Prince George in central British Columbia) because the Atlin Board of Trade decided that Indians should no longer go to the local school. She didn't go home for three full years because it was cheaper for the Department of Indian Affairs to keep the children in Lejac during the summer than to escort them home to Atlin. The unhappiness of those days has lingered and has sorely affected her adult life.

Such relentless proselytizing was epitomized by Father Allard who, in 1906, was sent to build a Catholic mission at Conrad on the Windy Arm of Tagish Lake. The town soon became deserted after the mining rush abated, so he moved to Atlin where he noted with disapproval "the greater number of Indians present at Easter Mass belonged to the Russian church." Presumably, this was because of the influence from the Russian fishing colonies on the coast near Angoon. Chief Taku Jack, Jennie's grandfather, learned his prayers from a Russian priest in Juneau.

A constant rivalry and skirmishing for souls existed between the Catholic and Protestant churches. Father Allard started a boarding school in Atlin, where he fed and taught the children while their parents went hunting. In return, the Indians provided him with moose meat. When he heard that a Protestant minister was in Teslin, he went there to try to avert competition. The Anglican minister in Conrad made a foray into Atlin where he begged the natives to let him have their children.

Tlingit society had a sophisticated structure and tradition. An established nobility and social rank existed, even though the number of people in the clans was small. Girls were secluded at puberty, some people practiced witchcraft and Satanism, and they held elaborate funeral potlatches. At potlatches, Crows would caw and Wolves would howl, each wearing appropriate emblems embroidered on ceremonial cloaks. The last known shaman of the Atlan Tlingit, Dr. Jackson, was reputedly more than 100 years old and had straggly hair that he refused to cut because he believed that, like Samson, his strength lay therein. One night, Father Allard crept up on Dr. Jackson when he was asleep and cut off his hair. The shaman died three days later.

In 1929, Father Allard's order published *Le Patriote de l'Ouest*, which includes a chapter entitled "Chez les Sauvages – La mission d'Atlin dans la Colombie Brittanique," euphemistically translated as "The natives at home." I own and treasure a book about the Moravian Missions in Labrador, published at the turn of the eighteenth century, wherein the natives, Inuit and Indian alike, are collectively and exclusively referred to throughout as "the heathen." Sadly, the patronizing attitude of the church towards aboriginals is an historical fact worldwide.

The Tlingits named most places on the upper Taku River, where they used to fish for salmon. Occasionally, they forayed over the divide into the Yukon River basin to trap for furs, especially marten and beaver. They fished with nets made of goat hair, set lines of hooks made from animal bone, and caught salmon in traps and speared them from the bank. When hunting beaver, they bored a

Tlingit family at their hunting camp. *(Vancouver Public Library, No. 12838)*

hole in the ice near a beaver house and, using a pole, shoved down a net made from strips of moose hide, called babiche. Then they scared the beaver into the net by beating on the roof and shaking a rattle made of dried moose hoof. Moose were hunted by setting a snare of moose hide over a hole in a fence built across a game trail and then calling the moose. They also made a deer-call whistle of green willow split in half with a grass reed held across it. When hunting goats, they would leave an item of clothing on an open hillside to fix the attention of the goat and then approach it from the rear.

The demand for inland furs grew during the eighteenth century, because the coastal sea otters had been hunted almost to extinction by European sailors. The coastal Chilkat Indians monopolized trade with the white traders and became middlemen between those traders and the inland Indians. They would travel through the interior to buy furs and sell, for huge profits, guns, tobacco, and liquor, and they would occasionally stay for a winter and take Tlingit

wives. But the inland Tlingit were disdainful of their coastal cousins, saying, "They don't know the land around here and they can't
go alone in the country. They're just like white people."

Eventually white people came to settle in the northwest. In
1840, Mr. James Douglas travelled north to find a site for a Hudson's Bay Company post at the mouth of the Taku, then still in
Russian-owned Alaskan territory. He reported that

*The higher elevations elsewhere were covered with ice and snow, the
lower levels with grasses and flowering plants in full bloom. So strangely
beautiful was the contrast between heavenly desolation and earthly paradise.
Yet swift and dangerous was the current, moreover being blocked by ice
during the winter.*

Douglas finally decided to place the fort 20 miles south of the
present Taku Harbour and across from Admiralty Island. Settlers
threw up pickets and blockhouses and fired a salute on the Fourth
of July. Douglas wrote:

*Trading began, but it was not wholly satisfactory, the savages being so
absorbed in dealing with slaves brought from a distance and used in com-
merce as a sort of currency, that they had few skins left to buy whiskey with.*

At the end of the nineteenth century, the Taku Tlingits became
guides and packers for prospectors and explorers. But the influx of
people into the region made it difficult for them to control the
movements of outsiders between the coast and the interior. Not to
be outdone by their coastal brethren, the Taku Tlingit chief allowed
each prospector to enter with 10 cents worth of tobacco and
enough money to buy caribou hide for clothing repairs. As the
prospectors left the area, the chief inspected their furs and charged
a tax on them.

Gradually, however, white people took control of the region, virtually subjugating the Indians. In June 1915, a British Columbian Royal Commission on Indian Affairs met with the Atlin Board of Trade to discuss the "Indian Town." Major Neville, the erstwhile water delivery man, opened his address:

The Board of Trade wants the Indians moved to some further spot than where they are now because it is part of the surveyed town. At some future date, it might be required for white people. A lot of the Indians are very unhealthy and we don't think it right that they should be so close to town. They simply came and squatted there when we white men came.

Jules Eggert spoke next:

The Indians have been approached and are perfectly willing to move if they get a reserve. B. O. T suggests Five Mile Point, as fine a place as could be got anywhere. Our intention is not to push the Indians out; we want them to have a proper place to live. But we don't like to have them in our midst. A great many of the Indians make this headquarters when they come down for their potlatch and generally they are accompanied by a large number of starving curs. We have tried to get them to feed their dogs, but they prefer to let them rustle. They are known to walk into a kitchen and steal meat or a pot of hot soup.

Captain Hathorne then said:

The missionaries have taken a great deal of trouble to educate and bring up these Indians. They have proved themselves useful, as everyone can testify, when we had a large fire here, and, really, I myself consider they are quite an asset to the place. But still it is the desire of the majority of the community that they be farther away.

The Indian agent Scott Simpson pointed out that the Indians were averse to being removed from their present abode. Next day,

Taku Jack (right) and group at Five Mile Point, 1903. *(Yukon Archives/Atlin Historical Society Collection, p.460)*

the Commission met with Chief Taku Jack and asked him to show on a map any special piece of land the Indians wanted to keep for themselves.

"I cannot read, and I don't know anything about a map," replied Chief Taku Jack. "You know how big the land is, and I know it because it belongs to me. This is the only country we have, and this is my country. You got no land to give me. I don't want to kick about the white people coming here. If they want to go prospecting, let them go. We're just like one brother, just as though we're eating off one table. I used to think I could get work out of the white people, but I never did because the Japs (sic) are working here on the creeks and we can do nothing. This little piece of land that you're trying to give us it wouldn't do us very good."

In the end, after much to and fro, the Commissioner suggested that perhaps the Indians should settle down, forego their nomadic hunting ways, and turn to farming and gardening instead. He offered the enticement of a school. Chief Taku Jack signed an agreement on behalf of the Atlin Band whereby the Indians were given several parcels of land: 160 acres on McDonald Lake for a fishing station, 120 acres on Coleman Lake for hay, 1,965 acres at Five Mile Point, a cemetery near Atlin, 160 acres on Silver Salmon Lake, and various small plots around Teslin Lake, but not the land where the Indian village stands and on which, by law, they are squatters.

A glance at a map of the Atlin region shows these designated Indian reserve lands to be a tiny part of the whole area where once they roamed free: hunting, trapping, and fishing, and uninhibited by imposed boundaries. The present-day Taku River Tlingits understand that their ancestors were cheated. The foreshore of the Indian village, where they have beached their boats since the turn of the century, is now owned by a summer resident white man who operates a boat rental business and a recreational vehicle campground. So they don't even have legal access to the beach in front of their own houses.

Chief Taku Jack said it all before: "The government say they don't allow the Indians to kill blue grouse and the birds we used to live on. So the Indians leave them [the birds] alone, but the white men kill them."

Despite their many disadvantages, some of the Indians were able to compete with whites on their own terms. Chief Taku Jack had several children among whom were Johnny, Leo, and Henry Taku Jack. As a boy, Johnny Taku Jack worked doing odd jobs in Atlin for Schulz and Pillman. Then he moved to Carcross where he got a job on a White Pass railroad gang. After that, he worked the river boats for five years as a deck hand splicing cable. When the mate was forced to retire because of illness, he walked over to Johnny and put on him his own brass-buttoned coat and hat as a sign of transfer. Johnny eventually quit the company to go prospecting with his brother Henry Taku Jack. Leo Taku Jack was a driver of one of the dog sleds that carried the mail.

The modern-day Jack family has proved itself no less remarkable.

SUMMER

Lake Sail

In the north, summer explodes out of spring with no gentle transition. When it's upon us, much has to be packed into the four months from June to September, so we try not to waste a minute — especially of the short sailing season.

Soon after we arrived in the Yukon, five friends and I ordered a spanking-new Northwest 21-foot sailboat to be shipped from Vancouver on a White Pass cargo freighter. We decided unanimously to keep the boat at Atlin because it was the best local sailing water and moorage. After a couple of years, I bought out the other partners and named the boat *Ven* (after a similar-sized, much-loved boat I had once owned on the River Dart in England).

I sank an engine block in the lee of First Island and chained a buoy to it. This side of the island, sheltered and in full view of the town, is where Atlin's tiny sailing fleet is moored. The island angles slightly to the prevailing southerlies and is covered with spruce trees. Above the trees projects a windsock to warn of wild storms that can suddenly produce wind gusts, or wiliwaws, which spiral off the surrounding mountains and howl down the lake. A ramshackle hut and the rails of a launching dolly are the remnants of a former float plane base.

Three other sail boats were moored there — all kept close to the island to stay out of the way of float planes that need to land in the leeward still water. The most handsome boat on the lake, *Arctic Tern*, was an Ericson 25, owned by Herman Peterson. A trimaran, *Wild Onion*, used to belong to George Esquiro, a Taku River Tlingit who, with no thought for black clouds brewing, would sail with the leeward pontoon digging into the water and the rigging howling like taut violin strings. The smallest boat was Harold Colwell's full keel sloop, *Bluebird*. Lying among the sail boats was Jack Weltzin's Boston Whaler lifeboat, her splayed bow giving her speed in foul weather.

Ven was designed as a day-sailer for a calm outing in Vancouver Harbour. Her shapely hull has adequate beam and a large cockpit. When the drop-keel is raised, she only draws 20 centimetres.

Adventurous crew are hard to find, so usually I sail singlehanded. Because I may have to shorten sail quickly on my own, I make a rule always to reef when whitecaps appear on the lake. It is much easier to shake out a reef than to go up on the fore deck to change jibs with the boat bouncing, sails flapping, and sheets thrashing around one's ankles.

My sailing and boat-building cohort was Harald Lawrence, a German electrical engineer from Hamburg. He and his wife, Hilke, came to Atlin after a holiday in Alaska, bought a lake shore plot that is located north of town with a panoramic view, and built an alpine chalet log house. Harald's left cheek is dented from a shrapnel wound that he received while fighting on the Russian Front in World War II; it looks like a duelling scar. His long, thin fingers are knobby at the joints from arthritis, which interferes with the fine use of his hands. His meticulous, obsessive craftsmanship is evident in his house; every joint fits perfectly. He hoards scrap odds and ends, and no tool is out of place in his workshop.

Harald and I agreed that in return for helping maintain *Ven* he could use her whenever I was not in Atlin. He is experienced in the vagaries of sail boats, having owned an ocean racer that he cruised all over the Baltic. He ordered the parts necessary to replace some worn rigging, and when they arrived we paddled out to inspect *Ven*.

"This is unimpossible. Oh, my dear, my dear," muttered Harald, as he sat hugging his toolbox in our small inflatable dinghy, which had only a thumbs breadth of freeboard. "Absolutely unimpossible."

In fact, we made it safely out to the moorage without shipping any water and took the necessary measurements.

One evening, we hauled *Ven* out of the water to fix the rigging. Harald was giving orders from his truck while I steered her onto the trailer — a difficult job in a crosswind. Harald drove swiftly forward to align truck and trailer before backing it up against the Harper Reed dock. I had just jumped off the trailer when an explosion overhead and a crackling blue flash announced that the top of the mast had cut a main power line. The masthead wind indicator welded itself to the electric cable and remained thus for many years. Guests at the nearby Kirkwood Cabins were in the middle of cooking supper and putting their children to bed. I shamefacedly phoned the manager of B.C. Hydro to report the incident and to apologize for making it necessary to call a lineman out on a weekend. I must confess that we repeated the same mistake, in an almost identical manner, two years later.

Other islands lie beyond First Island. Second Island is freehold property. No one is quite sure how it gained such status, because the other two islands are Crown Land and, thus, cannot be sold. Second Island has a few trees and a hillock in the middle, tucked into the lee of which is a good site for a cabin. Third Island is the largest of the three. Fourth Island is the rocky nubbin of a huge underwater reef that shows at low water; in midsummer high water, it lurks invisible — a light-coloured rock that looms like a surfacing monster. When the north end of Third Island is in line with the Glaciological Institute, we know we are somewhere near Fourth Island and that we should beware.

In spring, Charlie "Billy Goat" Brown used to load his goats into a rowboat and take them to pasture on Third Island. He would return to collect them in the fall. A New Zealander, Charlie farmed at Thron Gulch and mined in Atlin for over forty years.

Third Island was a favourite place for us to picnic with the children, and it was a safe hideaway where they could camp on their own when they became more daring. The farther side is out of sight of town and makes you feel as though you are alone in the middle of the lake — the sort of place for a latter-day Robinson Crusoe adventure.

One weekend, Sarah and I sailed over to the small, rounded bay at the north end of the island with Judith and Lucy. The shore is steep, so we nosed the boat right up to the beach and, having first dropped a stern anchor, tied it to a pine tree. The girls had assembled their camping gear from elaborate lists made at home. Lucy's started "spare pair knickers (in case we laugh too much)." We set up camp on a flat spot among juniper bushes. The site looked straight across to Torres Channel and the three rocky bastions of Atlin Mountain.

Sarah and I sailed back to town as the girls tried to light a fire to heat their baked beans. A pre-arranged signal in case of emergency was to be a sleeping bag hung over a low tree. We spied the bay through binoculars from the cabin but saw no sign of the sleeping bag. Next morning we returned and heard excited tales of the night's camping that grew many fold with the telling.

"Let's go on a bear hunt," I suggested. We each picked up a stick as a pretend gun and crept stealthily along the far side of the island, where a small cliff fell to the lake. Already excited by their camping adventure, the children were now tuned to fever pitch.

"Keep your heads down," I said. "We're in bear country. Now, very quiet, because the bear usually sleeps at the far end of the island, and we don't want to wake him."

Crawling gun-in-hand was difficult, and the closer we got to the end of the island, the more excited the children became. The very tip is rocky and extends into a treacherous reef.

"You guys go ahead and search the point," I whispered. "I'll stay here and guard our rear in case the bear creeps up on us from the woods."

The children edged forward in silence, staring wide-eyed with anticipation. I hid behind a boulder and watched them creeping over the rocks. Finding nothing on the point, they turned around and approached my hiding place. I gave a low growl that brought them to a dead halt. I gave another, louder growl, and they vaulted into the air. When I emerged, they wailed and giggled hysterically, their eyes tearful and their knickers wet. We walked back along the island, climbing over broken stumps and through thick trees beside a small slough where ducks were nesting.

We all sailed back to town. The girls spines were still atingle with their adventure, which they recounted dramatically to Sarah. The event has passed into family folklore.

The first year we owned our sailboat, the whole family prepared to sail down to the south end of the lake to explore the islands and glaciers hidden from Atlin by Teresa Island. Adam and I rowed across to *Ven's* mooring. He was becoming a handy crew, though his sisters were less than enthusiastic as soon as the boat began to heel even a few degrees.

"Dad, stop the boat side-lopping," they would cry. "We can see water through the window. Make it stand up straight."

We raised the jib and main and sailed across the town bay to tie up to the dock in front of Kirkwood's cabins. Sarah and the girls came aboard and stowed the food and camping gear for a week's journey. *Ven* slept two people comfortably: the skipper on a wide bunk in the belly of the ship and the crew on a quarter berth on the starboard side — a constant catalyst to mutiny. A triangular berth in the bow fitted one child, or two at a pinch, so we also took a tent to pitch on shore.

Since it was late in the day, we sailed over to Third Island to camp for the night. We would make a Hudson's Bay start in the morning. In the old days, when setting out on a long dog sled journey, Hudson's Bay Company employees would leave in the evening and camp on the outskirts of town. Since everything was organized the night before and it was not necessary to mess about with half-remembered matters on the morning of departure, this practice ensured a full-day's travel on the first day.

The following morning, the lake was free of whitecaps, so we dressed *Ven* in a full suit of sails. After several tacks, we cleared the reef that hangs between the end of First Island and the point in front of the Catholic church where the Taku Tlingits beach their boats. Father Plaine waved to us from his study window in the rectory.

Winds on the lake are capricious. A stiff breeze usually blows out of Torres Channel and meets the south wind that chases down the length of the lake, creating turbulence just beyond Third Island. It often pays to tack early, head into Pine Creek Bay, and then tack again to make Five Mile Point.

We sailed close-hauled towards Six Mile Bay on Teresa Island where lies a submerged reef that I had noted from the air. It is prudent to assume that every island in the lake bears a southward-trailing reef, but there are many more that lie uncharted, waiting to take a bite out of the hull of a careless skipper's boat. As they say in Newfoundland, "Oi don't know wur all them reefs is, bye, but oi knows wur they bain't."

Atlin Lake has never been properly charted. On a calm spring day, when the lake was at its lowest level, Herman Peterson and I flew the shoreline at 1,000 feet in his Luscombe float plane so I could take photos of all the islands and dangerous reefs with the lake at its lowest level. Arden Hixson did the same in his plane, and thus we collected a useful reference volume of photos. According to their depth below the surface, the reefs change colour from deep azure

to green to pale yellow. I marked them on a 1:50,000 topographical map which became my home-made navigational chart.

Approaching Six Mile Bay's white sandy beach head-on, we
dropped an anchor over the stern and luffed into the wind to lose
speed. If you let go too early, the anchor line runs out and jerks the
boat to a halt before reaching shore. Worse still is forgetting to wind
up the centreboard. If it bites into the bottom, you have to turn
around, sail out into the bay, and repeat the approach.

Ven crunched gently against the shore, and Adam jumped over
the bow pulpit and passed a mooring line round a tree. Then he
passed the line back to Judith who took a turn round a cleat. We
pulled on the aft anchor line to float the boat again, so that the hull
would not rub on the sand and adjusted the bow line so that the
boat would hold steady. Harald Lawrence had made a simple
wooden ladder of two-by-twos which Adam propped against the
bow so that Sarah and the girls could step off easily with the boxes
of food and cooking gear.

We made a fire in a communal pit, and steaks soon sizzled on
a grill made from the stainless steel shelf of a discarded fridge. The
children pitched the tent on a flat area under some trees so that they
could enjoy the adventure of being on their own, well away from
their parents. Nearby, trout swam upstream towards a waterfall on
a creek that flowed from the upper slopes of Birch Mountain. The
sun settled behind the three chunky peaks of Atlin Mountain. In
bygone aeons, a nearby volcano blew its top and Mount Minto was
left alone to guard the portals to the north. From wherever you
look, its pyramidal shape rises from its broad base to its shoulders.
Then it angles gently to the summit.

At night, we moved the boat out farther in case the wind shifted
and blew her towards the shore. Sarah and I slept aboard with a
mosquito net stretched across the cabin hatchway. Making amends
for the long dark days of winter, the sun still provided enough light
to read a book without a flashlight at midnight. Next morning, we
raised sail and tacked towards Twelve Mile Point, which is further

along the same shore of Teresa Island. There, we made breakfast. The scar of the McKee Creek mine workings stood out on the mainland opposite. To the south, the exit stream from the Warm Springs indented the shoreline of Warm Bay.

As we neared the middle of the lake, I recalled vividly a sunny Saturday afternoon a few weeks before when I had been out alone sailing *Ven* around Third Island. An ominous black cloud had darkened the skies over Twelve Mile Point, and the wind had risen, sending whitecaps racing down the lake. I had scuttled for my mooring.

Back on the deck of our cabin, Sarah and I had watched the anticipated storm arrive. Waves whipped past the islands. Meanwhile, a tragic drama was unfolding below the black cloud yonder. Two tourists, Jane and Ray, had sailed their Klepper kayak from Warm Bay across to Teresa Island for a picnic. They were accompanied by a friend, along with his young son and a dog, who had paddled across in an open canoe. In worsening weather, they had decided to return the three miles to Warm Bay before the lake became too rough. The wind grew strong and erratic, and a black cloud hovered over them. The canoeist made a direct line for shore, but, because of the head wind, the kayakers could not head straight for Warm Bay. They tried to tack. Soon they were swamped in the breaking waves. Baling was futile. Twenty minutes later the Klepper capsized in the middle of the lake.

Being dunked in cold water was a shock to Ray and Jane. They both had flotation jackets. Jane also wore a down vest, a heavy Cowichan wool sweater, and jeans, but Ray had only jeans and a shirt. They tried to right the kayak but failed because of the stepped mast hanging down in the water. So, holding on as best they could and trying to keep their bodies out of the water, which felt much colder than the air, they straddled the bottom of the boat. Ray, against the advice of Jane, swam to keep warm. Jane huddled quite still with her knees drawn up, wrapped a small tarpaulin around her head, and lashed her wrists to the boat.

Violent shivering wracked her, but it stopped after forty-five minutes — an ominous sign that her nervous system could no longer generate heat by causing her muscles to contract involuntarily. Her mind began to slip and her strength waned, but she felt no pain or cold. She heard choking as Ray drifted away from the boat. Then he made no further sound.

Their friend in the canoe had seen from afar that the kayak was in trouble, but he was having extreme difficulty paddling against the wind and waves. So he headed to Warm Bay to summon help — an hour's paddle in those conditions. There, he met a tourist who immediately sent a message to the RCMP on his mobile radio. Then the tourist launched his aluminum boat, powered with a five horsepower outboard motor, and headed off into the teeth of the storm towards the scene of the accident. On reaching the upturned Klepper, he hauled Jane on board his own small craft — a difficult manoeuvre in the rough water.

The helicopter arrived soon after, by which time Jane had been in the water for about two and a half hours. The pilot hovered over the boat while his engineer stood on the skid and tried to reach down to Jane, but the downward draft of the rotor blades threatened to swamp the aluminum boat. The pilot returned to the sawmill at Warm Bay and collected a hemp rope, which he lowered to the man in the boat who tied it under Jane's arms with the knot against her chest. Jane was slung to shore, where she was transferred to the back of the helicopter. There, the engineer tried to restrain her as she thrashed about wildly.

Hearing a commotion of helicopter blades, Sarah, who is a nurse, and I hurried over to the Atlin outpost nursing station. Jane arrived raving, struggling violently, and frothing at the mouth. Her muscles were stiff with cold. We put her into the bath fully clothed and added hot tap water to keep the temperature close to 44 degrees Celsius. She breathed in gasps, her pulse was rapid and erratic, her pupils widely dilated, and her eyes vacant. After being rewarmed for about an hour, she calmed down so that we could undress her and it became much easier to keep her in the bath. Her rectal temperature was 35 degrees Celsius; it took an hour to rise to normal.

The nursing station hot water tank ran dry, so we moved Jane to the Atlin Inn, which had plenty of hot water. She was thirsty and her muscles ached severely, so we kept her in a warm bath for a further two hours. At this point, she was so improved that we were able to cancel plans to fly her to Whitehorse. Jane spent the night in the hotel with a girlfriend watching over her. She was physically quite stable, but her emotional pain was wicked. Later, she was able to give a lucid account of her ordeal.

Jane had survived at least two and a half hours in six to seven degrees Celsius water, close to the known limits of survival for those conditions, while Ray had lasted only 45 minutes. The balance was tipped in her favour because she had attended to small details remembered from a lecture on cold water survival she had attended a few weeks earlier. Her Cowichan pullover of heavy wool had insulated her better than most other materials that lose their insulation when wet, and she had covered her head, from where half the body heat is lost. By remaining still she had avoided burning calories in fruitless attempts to swim; at ten degrees Celsius, a normal person can swim about a kilometre before succumbing to hypothermia. Huddling in a crouched position had reduced heat loss from blood vessels lying close to the surface of her armpits and groins. By climbing on top of the upturned boat, she had reduced her time in contact with the very cold water. Tying herself on had prevented her from drifting away from the boat and made her more likely to be spotted.

Women generally have more body fat than men and are thereby better insulated — an advantage to Jane despite her spare build. Ray's futile attempts to swim to keep warm, his inadequate clothing, and his lean body had all mitigated against his survival.

Despair can be overwhelming in shipwreck. In despair, victims tend to neglect small details that may tip the balance and allow them to survive. Jane did everything right.

The tragedy made me sharply aware of the hazards of sailing on the icy waters of Atlin Lake, especially single-handedly. With this in mind, Harald and I later adapted *Ven's* rigging to bring all the reefing lines back to the cockpit. Changing head sails on the fore deck in a blow can be a nightmare, because the boat bucks, sails flap wildly, and the boom is liable to whip across and knock one unconscious into the water. With roller reefing on the jib, I could reef the boat in less than a minute without the need of going forward on deck.

With these sobering thoughts in mind, we sailed towards the large island that guards Twelve Mile Bay. On the east side, a small rock stood in the middle of a narrow fairway, so Adam and I took short tacks to reach the sheltered bay beyond. We aimed for an outcrop at one end of the long sandy beach, avoiding a submerged reef where a beaver had built a house. The marks of his teeth were on many of our firewood sticks, which had been washed up at high water. Ashore, Sarah soon had the kettle boiling, and bacon and eggs crackled in the frying pan. The wind bent the tree tops and moaned in the upper branches; wild weather awaited us round the point.

Across the bay and beside a stream, stood a small cabin with a corrugated iron roof. It was used as a fishing camp in summer and as a base for a trap line in winter. Judith and Lucy led us on a half-hour hike along a flat moss- and lichen-covered trail that passed though big trees, bush willow, tussock grass, and bog. We reached the edge of a small lake where a couple of loons called to each other with their mellifluous, haunting cry.

After breakfast, we loaded the grub boxes back into the well of the cabin, untied from the tree, and climbed aboard. Adam pulled up the ladder, and I hauled on the anchor rope so that we would clear the beach before raising sail. These tricky manoeuvres are best practiced without relying on an engine in case one day the engine quits and we have to manage without power. A few thrills in the safe confines of Atlin harbour is fun, but the middle of a very cold, vicious, lonely lake is no place to practice. Seeing whitecaps around the corner, we went into the shelter of a leeward bay, put up the sturdy storm jib and reefed the mainsail. This avoided the nightmare of being out in the middle of the lake with sails flapping, the boat pitching, bucking, and heeling with the lee rail under water, and wife and children wailing in protest.

Rounding Twelve Mile Point, the wind blowing off the Llewellyn Glacier thwacked us. But the little boat, doubly-reefed and with the pocket-handkerchief storm jib, heeled comfortably. We tacked across to the shallow mouth of Pike River, where the Telegraph Trail emerges from Nakina country to the east. Passing under the lee of Merry's Island, we put in to a sheltered moorage against a small shingly spit. Straddling the neck of this little horse-shoe-shaped island is Wayne's Pond, which is so shallow that at midsummer the water becomes warm enough to swim in — unlike the rest of the lake. We lit a fire of tinder-crisp spruce twigs to warm ourselves and, laying a soot-encrusted pot on a grate across a couple of logs, we soon had steaming mugs of tea in our hands.

The wind moderated, so Adam shook out the reef and we pulled up anchor and set off. We were aiming for Caribou Island and Peggy's Cove, which lay across the widest part of the lake. At the far end of the channel, where a scant, fluky wind blew down of the slopes of Birch Mountain, a pencil of smoke rose from the trees; Peggy Milius was at home.

Ahead, on a gravel spit surrounded by deep water, stood a short figure waving her arms in welcome. Moored in a round bay behind her lay a raft, upon which stood a large canvas wall tent decorated with hand-painted loons. We dropped a stern anchor and nestled up close to her houseboat.

Visiting at Peggy's Cove.

"Good to see you," said Peggy. "Come ashore and tie up to that
tree. There's never any wind in here. I'll put on a kettle." She stirred
the smouldering embers in a stone fire pit beside which was a neat
pile of split wood.

Short and grandmotherly like Mrs. Tiggywinkle, Peggy's grey-
ing hair was curled in an untidy bun on the crown of her head. Her
eyes glinted through thick spectacles. She was dressed in trousers,
a loose shirt, and a canvas sailor's smock with her sleeves rolled to
her elbows. Her casual appearance was in keeping with living for
many weeks away from civilization.

"Let me show you around," she said as she walked up the gangplank. "I designed and built her. This platform's made of two-by-
twelve lumber. It rests on thirty oil drums that John Thoma bolted
into place. He also welded the paddle-wheel and fixed the motor."

A narrow walkway led round to the stern, where a Toyota truck
engine was mounted sideways with a heavy chain linking the crank-
shaft to the paddle-wheel.

"I just put her in gear, forward or reverse, and away I go," said Peggy. She didn't mention any of her tempestuous solo journeys, now folklore in Atlin, down to her summer moorage. A ship's wheel, linked to three rudders, was mounted aft of the paddle-wheel. The best way to steer the heavy raft was to quarter crab-like into the wind, but this was neither comfortable or safe when following the rocky lee shore of Teresa Island. A canoe hung from davits on one side as a token lifeboat; on the other side were storage boxes and a punting pole.

"Let's go inside and have a drink," said Peggy. She poured the tea and took some milk from the propane fridge set under a wooden frame to the left of the door. "I'm expecting Herman Peterson to fly in with some mail. Perhaps he'll replenish my Scotch. It's getting a bit low. I'm having such a lovely summer. Hardly any visitors, so I'm doing lots of painting. Boo Curelly's coming for a week soon, and she'll stay in the guest tent up on the lookout. I love having company, but not for too long as it interrupts my painting."

Peggy's oil paintings mainly depict evocative scenes of the lake and its distant glaciers. Her previous career as an interior designer was evident in her tent furniture, built of weathered pine boards collected from an old barn in Discovery. Against the right-hand wall stood a counter and sink. She raised water from the lake by means of an old-fashioned cast-iron pump with an elegantly curved handle. The knobs on the kitchen cabinets were made of moose antler secured by leather thongs. A couch with fitted cushions became a bed by night. Above it, a bookcase held the two volumes of the Shorter Oxford English Dictionary and a row of books that reflected Peggy's wide interests. On the left side of the tent, an oval Yukon stove and a bake-oven stood in a shallow hearth of pebbles with a box of split wood nearby. The stovepipe passed through a tin fireguard sewn into the canvas roof. Beside the entrance doorway, a wooden shower stall doubled as a hanging closet. The sun heated her shower water, contained in a heavy, black plastic bag on the tent roof.

"I lived in California for many years," said Peggy. " And then I came to Atlin. I doubt I'll ever leave."

When Peggy first started spending her summers down the lake, she made camps on several different islands. Each campsite was lovingly chosen and crafted. She would build a tent platform, a fireplace, and the limited essentials to make a comfortable camp for three or four months. These islands became known as Peggy's Islands — One, Two, Three, and so on — as she moved around the lake to find different views to paint.

"There are so many Peggy's Islands, I'd better give you one," she said. "Come on up to the bluff, and I'll show you which it is." We followed a winding path through the forest and past her guest tent, strung from a frame of spruce poles. From a small cliff facing the Llewellyn Glacier, we gazed over the myriad islands of the south end of Atlin Lake.

"It's due south over there between Bastion and Griffith Islands," she said, pointing to an dumbbell-shaped island. "Approach from this side and you'll find a sheltered moorage. But watch out for a submerged rock in the middle of the bay."

And so it became Steele Island. So poorly charted is the lake that such eponyms are common. We gazed towards our newly-acquired domain from a seat nailed into the fork of a gnarled pine.

"I once had to climb that tree to escape a bear, so I hammered those nails in to make it easier." said Peggy. "He just became too inquisitive for my own good. He wandered over from the salt lick in the slough over there. In the morning, when there's mist on the lake, I often see moose drinking in the cove. Occasionally there's a bear, but usually they keep their distance."

The children explored the headland, a place redolent of island adventures, while Sarah and I walked back to the boat with Peggy. As we prepared to sail we heard the drone of an engine. A small yellow float plane with orange markings circled overhead and, throwing up a wave of spray, landed in the bay. After taxiing to the beach of the spit beside *Ven*, out climbed the pilot, a man with grey crinkly hair and a grizzled weather-beaten face.

"Emergency rations," said Herman Peterson laconically as he handed Peggy a long brown paper bag.

We took our leave, and as we sailed out into the lake, we all waved good-bye to Peggy.

After our visit with Peggy, we headed towards Cannonball Island offshore of Griffith. Beyond lay Steele Island, its two rocky promontories, one higher than the other, separated by a neck of land. In the entrance channel of the protected cove was a barely submerged reef, its rocky head prominent at spring low water. We avoided it, moored to a tree on the beach, and threw an anchor astern.

Twenty metres across the island, a stony beach faced the south prevailing wind. Tangled driftwood lay at the high watermark. Adam lit a fire in the fire pit of Peggy's old campsite, which was located in an open space among the trees. Judith and Lucy wanted to camp alone in the tent, so Sarah, Adam, and I sailed to a neighbouring cove on Bastion Island, about a kilometre away.

From our anchorage in a narrow passage between rocky cliffs, we raised and lowered our jib three times. The girls responded from the island with three flashlight signals.

Next day, we sailed back to Steele Island before a rising wind unleashed the fury of a full gale. We joined the girls, ecstatic after their lone adventure, and cooked breakfast while a force six wind howled through the treetops. When the storm abated, we hoisted sail and crossed towards Lake Inlet, which cuts deep into the rocky mountainside below the Llewellyn Glacier. Adam put out a line from the back of the boat and caught a big lake trout. On shore, we cleaned the fish, wrapped it in wet newspaper and cooked it in the embers of a fire.

We hiked the trail that approached the Llewellyn Glacier from the head of Lake Inlet. After an hour of meandering through thick forest, we reached the glacial flood plain from where we saw the toe of the icefall. The contorted geography of glaciers is generally best seen from the air, looking down on the shadowed relief of crevasses created by the moving river of ice, rather than looking up at the mucky foreshortened toe of a moraine.

We sailed round to Llewellyn Inlet where our Tlingit friend George Esquiro was skimming his wind surfer in a strong wind that rolled in gusts off the cliffs. He had left his brother Tom, a professional helicopter pilot but no sailor, to single-handedly sail his trimaran.

George, a fanatical sailor, was always out in his boat *Wild Onion,* unreefed in the wildest weather. He could cross the lake at double the speed of *Ven* — partly because of larger sail area, but mostly because of seamanship. George had ambitions for a bigger boat, so he went south and bought *Arrogant*, a 42-foot racing sloop, in a boatyard where she was growing weeds and barnacles. He sailed her up the Inland Passage to Skagway and berthed her there over the winter.

Soon after, I met him in Whitehorse, and he invited me to race with him round Admiralty Island, off Juneau, Alaska. He had a throw-together crew, a boat in need of a coat of paint, no new sails nor a spinnaker, and a huge black Bouvier dog, Dipper, who occupied most of the cockpit. To the amazement of the sleek armada of competing American yachts, *Arrogant* surged forward, with the wind strong on her nose. On the first leg from Juneau to Baranoff Hot Springs, we bucked a gale to come in second place, splitting our genoa because George refused to shorten sail.

I sewed the sail with surgical thread, and George produced a bottle of lucky Taku River water, brought from Tulsequah by his cousins who were salmon fishing there. He drank some, poured the rest into the sea, and within minutes a breeze came up and pushed us to the head of the fleet. Dolphins danced alongside. A humpback whale rose and blew not ten metres from the boat, dived with its bifid flukes rising out of the water like two supplicant hands, and then slid back into the depths. To starboard lay Angoon, the Tlingit fishing capital, and to port was Peril Straight, which leads to Sitka. We crossed the finish line at Auke Bay in second place, but we took the trophy because we had the best aggregate points for the two days of racing.

George skippered *Arrogant* in his own modest style: no shouting, few orders, and little organization. Things just worked out, as can only happen with such a quality seaman.

On the way out of Llewellyn Inlet, we met Wayne Merry in his voyageur canoe, paddled by half a dozen clients from his wilderness outfitting business. We exchanged greetings and swung across to Peggy's Other Island. It lay in the middle of the channel leading to Second Narrows, which separates Teresa Island from the mainland. Birch Mountain makes Teresa the world's highest freshwater island. First and Second Narrows encompass Copper Island; each channel is so slender that at low water a boat has to thread a very careful course. The *Tarahne* used to pass through Second Narrows on her round-the-island cruises in the 1930s. In midsummer, when the warmth of the sun melts snow on the hills, she could just squeeze through.

West lay the blind end of Williston Bay, where wind usually howls off the ice-cap down through a gap in the mountains and then dissipates halfway down Torres Channel. Fan-shaped glacial silt made a poor anchorage, so we sailed back and camped on a small island at the mouth of Second Narrows. The massive face of Cathedral Mountain towered above us. As I gazed up at the unclimbed face, my eye followed a line up the main rib, and I vowed to explore a route up it some day. I thought of our good fortune at being in this land in the golden era, such as Eric Shipton had known in the Himalayas in the 1930s, when few people had explored, let alone climbed, the mountains.

Sarah on the Arctic Tern, with Cathedral rising magnificently in the background.

Homeward bound, we ran before the wind down the length of Torres Channel. We rounded a small rocky point on the west side before Section Creek and found ourselves in a bowl-shaped moorage, where a steep beach led up to a sheltered flat area of grass. Ashore, Sarah lit a fire using a fistful of dry twigs snapped close to the trunk of a spruce tree and protected from rain by an umbrella of upper branches.

After lunch, we ran on down the channel. The following wind filled the sails, set wing-on-wing, jib on one side, mainsail on the other. The light air was perfect for the spinnaker, so Adam went forward to raise the sail as quickly as possible to prevent it from wrapping itself round the forestay like an hour-glass. The spinnaker ballooned out and we felt a surge of speed with every puff of wind, but we still kept a weather eye astern for sudden squalls.

In a bay nestled into the lower slopes of Atlin Mountain, a small log cabin was tucked into the trees. Each summer, Boo Curelly finds peace here from city life down east in Ontario. The cabin stands among scattered balsam and aspen trees on a flat spit of land and has a view of any boat traffic coming down Torres Channel. With the help of a strong Australian, Boo built a five- by seven-metre cabin out of squared logs. Inside, a single room is furnished with rough lumber. A ladder leads to a sleeping loft under a steep-pitched roof.

A spring snow avalanche had carved a swathe through the trees on Teresa Island opposite, like a razor's stroke across a stubbly beard. Everything in its path had been carried along on a tide of water-logged snow that knocked mature trees down like match sticks. When the ice thawed in summer, the debris of the snow slide, a huge pile of jumbled logs stripped bare of bark and limbed of branches, lay higgledy-piggledy like pick-up sticks far out into the lake. We sailed well clear, because submerged logs often hang ver-tically in the water and are difficult to see from the aft cockpit.

We dropped our sails well out and, keeping our rigging clear of an orange plane drawn up on the beach, drifted up to the small dock. Boo's daughter Judy was visiting from Atlin. She owns the plane, which she flies commercially; she is also a talented artist.

We all went ashore for tea and then set sail for Atlin. After an adventurous week away, the cabin seemed luxurious compared with the confined space of the boat. It was always a joy to return there, and it was comforting, when away, to know that the cabin, con-stant, unchanging and friendly, was waiting for us.

Adventures

Set in the heart of such wild country, Atlin attracts adventurous spirits. One day, I suggested to Wayne Merry that we try to scale the huge unclimbed face of Cathedral Mountain. We could see its dark triangle of rock looming far down Torres Channel. Wayne was well-qualified to tackle such a route. In 1958, he made the first ascent of The Nose of El Capitan, a colossal cliff in California's Yosemite Valley. That climb, done with maestro Warren Harding, became a benchmark in North American, and indeed world, rock climbing.

Martyn Williams and Selwyn Hughes, both physical education teachers in Whitehorse and good rock climbers, completed our team. We set off across the calm lake in Wayne's freighter canoe. Beyond Third Island, the wind suddenly rose, causing turbulent whitecaps.

The canoe plunged into each wave, and ice-cold spume sprayed back into the boat. Martyn, Selwyn, and I huddled under a tarpaulin for shelter while Wayne, in cold discomfort, operated the outboard motor from the stern. He slowed the canoe to avoid digging into the short choppy waves and quartered into the wind that was building into a major storm. To our right, waves broke on the rocky knob reef of Fourth Island. We searched hopefully across the lake for the mouth of Torres Channel three kilometres farther on and were glad to find shelter there.

The face of Cathedral Mountain loomed larger as we approached down the channel and, from its foot, we looked up six hundred metres of near vertical rock. A dozen fluted ridges plunged from the summit crest to the narrow fringe of trees that separated the mountain from blue water. We beached the canoe in a sandy bay and pitched camp among some spruce trees. From a rocky point nearby, we studied the face through binoculars in order to pick out the best route. A prominent ridge rose from the water's edge to the summit cone, making a smooth, classic line. We built a roaring fire on the beach and, ready for an alpine start before the next sunrise and excited by the adventure of exploring untrodden ground, turned into our sleeping bags after supper.

Our early-morning sleep was disturbed by the thwack of the rotor blades of a helicopter that settled farther along the beach. The pilot brought a message from one of my colleagues in Whitehorse; I was being asked to consult on a patient with a severe eye injury. My friends promised to await my return before starting the climb. They would spend the day exploring the best approach to the foot of the cliff.

The helicopter whapped hornet-like over the tree-tops and through mountain clefts on the way to the hospital. I operated on the patient's eye and, everything being satisfactory, returned to the camp by helicopter in mid-afternoon.

Next morning, we scampered up the lower slopes unroped on sound, gentle-angled rock. Soon the ridge steepened and became fractured, so we roped together in two pairs — Martyn with Selwyn and Wayne with me. Martyn, his tousled reddish hair and scrawny beard framing a determined face, moves with grace on difficult rock. Selwyn, tall and strong due to his blacksmith heritage in the Welsh coal valleys, was a reliable second on the rope. Wayne, to my comfort, was a rock-sure leader with vast experience on large rock faces.

Climbing Cathedral, with the vast expanse of Atlin Lake below.

Our spirits soared along with the eagles that rode the air currents rushing up the mountain face. There they hovered steady against the buffeting wind before diving off in smooth curving sweeps. We alternated lead positions. The second man was always firmly attached to the mountain by a rope belay. Blocks of rotten rock formed the unstable, knife-edge top of the ridge, so we trod with especial caution, testing every foot and handhold before putting weight on them. Chunks of mountain broke off despite our care. They rumbled down the vertical drops on either side and unleashed sparks as the disintegrating rock crashed towards the lake.

After eight hours of hard climbing and another hundred metres of steep rock, we reached the top. In the distance, jagged peaks stuck out of the Llewellyn Glacier, a contorted river of ice that spills off the Juneau Icecap and flows into a murky pool of glacial silt short of the foot of the lake. We looked at the vast empty landscape that stretched across the horizon and the island-spattered lake in the foreground. It was one of the most magnificent views I can recall in a lifetime of mountaineering. I remembered some lines I once read: "Unless you are a mountaineer, you may return to the grave without having ever know what it is like when the contour lines begin to sing together like the Biblical stars." We returned to Atlin deeply satisfied with our adventure. Whenever I look at the huge face of Cathedral Mountain, I recall that exciting day.

As a follow-up to our climb on Cathedral Mountain, I decided to paddle Pine Creek with Adam. I had done some paddling before coming to Canada, and soon after arriving in the Yukon, I had joined a small band of kayak enthusiasts. Before spring break-up, we had built our own kayaks out of fibreglass in a makeshift workshop. We learned our paddling skills during winter sessions in the swimming pool and by manoeuvering in the turbulent water below the Whitehorse powerhouse dam, where we practiced turn-outs, ferry-glides, and Eskimo rolls.

Generally, I prefer the companionship that a Canadian canoe offers, because teamwork is needed to guide a canoe down the best path through a rapid, whereas a kayak can turn on a dime. Kayaking is a more solitary occupation and very much less comfortable, because your legs are extended and there is no support for your back.

Pine Creek begins at the outlet of Surprise Lake. Its Tlingit name is Ku-sol-hin, which means narrow river. Having paddled this creek several times before, I knew that this name is a fitting one; steep hills fall sharply on all sides, and the river shoots under a log bridge, making an eddy pool below the pilings. We launched my new, supposedly unbreakable, Kevlar canoe and practiced a few strokes to find our sea-legs before venturing downstream.

The creek rippled for the first few kilometres and meandered through marshland, where ducks abounded. A bull moose, browsing on grass in the shallows, turned and ran off, its huge muscular legs thrashing through squelchy mud. As the river accelerated and bubbled over submerged rocks, a kaleidoscope of coloured stones shone from the river bottom. Small standing waves formed where water turned back on itself downstream of rounded boulders. The current undermined the bank and exposed roots of trees that would eventually keel over to form sweepers. If a canoe capsizes, these fallen trees can pin the legs of a paddler and drown him. We gave such sweepers a wide berth and hoped that the next floodwater would float them downstream.

In an eddy above one of the road bridges, we got out and scouted to make sure there was enough headroom under the bridge and no obstruction beyond it. The riverbanks were bright with yellow arnica mingled with silver lichen, and blue lupins grew in a widely-spaced pine forest, which allows more room for flowers to breathe than a crowded spruce forest. Dwarf alpine fireweed bloomed on the sandbars where we beached.

We approached the mine site of Discovery. At the turn of the century, this was a city of 5,000 people; now it was a jumbled mess of mining operations and tailings. The dredges of the Guggenheim company formed semi-circular berms. Ahead, I could hear the rush of turbulent water, so we beached in a quiet eddy, climbed the bank, and looked down into a small canyon where the creek cut a chute a hundred metres long. Anticipating a wild ride on the rolling stand-ing waves, we paddled out into mid-stream and headed for the smooth pillow of water sliding over the lip of the rapid. Beyond, we saw the foaming tops of breaking waves. Adam back paddled strongly, slowing the canoe and keeping it riding the waves, while I steered down the middle of the channel. A roar reverberated from the walls around us as we rushed headlong into the canyon. After a few seconds, we emerged into quiet water at the bottom.

We paddled on through water muddied by sluice box washings. Portaging around a waterfall, we stumbled over contorted Discovery tailings and stopped frequently to rest our shoulders and nurse stubbed toes. The stern paddler, head inside the upturned boat, stares at the footsteps of the person under the bow and curses when the leader trips. We were tramping over historic ground littered with

Miners at Never Miss Bench, Pine Creek. *(Yukon Archives/Atlin Historical Society Collection, p. 534)*

mining machinery of another age: sections of pipe, sluice box skeletons, engine parts, stake posts, and pit props.

Prospectors had explored the country around Atlin for several years before the rush that followed the discovery of gold on Pine Creek. On July 27, 1898 Fritz Miller and Kenny McLaren registered their discovery with Captain D'Arcy Strickland at the Tagish Lake North West Mounted Police post. Strickland, with eleven men, immediately went to Atlin, supposedly on business, and staked the ground surrounding the Discovery site for themselves. Discovery was thought to be in the Yukon and therefore bound by Yukon mining laws, which are different from those of British Columbia: a Yukon claim is 250 feet long; a British Columbia claim is 100 feet long. Sam Steele of the NWMP and Government Agent William Rant from Bennett went to Discovery and decided it was certainly in British Columbia — a fact that caused confusion in registering claims for years afterwards because of the difference in mining laws.

News of the Atlin strike quickly filtered back to Skagway. Hundreds of men in the White Pass & Yukon Railway workforce heard the news, quit, and headed off across Fantail Lake towards Atlin with hopes of making their fortunes. They pitched tents at Pine City, where a town site was surveyed. The numerous mining claims in the valley were staked so randomly that the mining ground could not be properly surveyed. Everyone who built a house or pitched a tent was illegally squatting on untitled land.

Despite the apparent chaos, a score of businesses operated out of tents, gamblers and hookers thrived in the hotels and saloons, and a stage coach ran daily between Discovery and Atlin. In 1899 the Alien Exclusion Act, which limited the issuing of miners' licences to British subjects only, was passed by the British Columbia Legislature. This sent many American miners packing in disgust. A decade later, the boom had bust, and Discovery became the ghost town it remains today.

As Adam and I stumbled across the boulders, our musings over these events of nearly a century before were overshadowed by our desire to complete the home stretch down river to Pine Creek Bridge. Overconfident, we failed to scout a blind corner where we suddenly came on a huge boulder surrounded by a ruff of white water.

"Draw hard!" I shouted. "Now paddle forward."

Sideways to the stream, we were swiftly approaching the rock. I forced my paddle against the gunwale and pushed the water away from the boat in order to move us into the line of the current, but the water was so powerful we couldn't turn the canoe. We hit the rock broadside amidships. Water poured over the gunwales and filled the canoe, which had wrapped itself around the rock. Standing waist deep in freezing snow-melt, we tried to pull one end free to empty out the water, but the canoe was firmly stuck.

We fixed a pulley using a rope sling around a tree, tied our climbing rope to a thwart, and gradually straightened the canoe so

Discovery (originally called Pine Town or Pine City) in 1900.
(Yukon Archives/Atlin Historical Society Collection, p.1026)

the water ran out. Righting the empty boat, we pulled her to shore to inspect the damage and were relieved to find no holes. A few well-placed kicks restored the Kevlar to shape. With such an insult, the back of any plastic or wood canoe would have been irreparably broken.

Our confidence shattered, we back paddled most of the difficult stretches down the river to slow us down and keep under control. A fence on the bank heralded Halfway House, where we ended our journey before the creek reached Pine Creek Bridge. Thereafter, the river follows a course of right-angled bends through a deep gorge where it tips over several high waterfalls and forms violent eddies; no boat or person could survive that stretch of water. The scars on the bottom of my shiny red canoe made it look as though some grizzly bear had fought with it. Red marks of Kevlar on the rocks upstream were a testimony to our adventure.

As we look out from the cabin, nearly every hilltop in our span of vision has at some time or other fallen under the tread of our boots. In late summer, well into the spirit of all our outdoor activities, the children and I sailed across the lake to climb Atlin Mountain.

We moored *Ven* at the mouth of a stream that drains from the scree slopes below the southern peak; we intended to do the climb and return to the boat in a day. Su-sun, the Tlingit name for the mountain, means pine cone. From our back porch, I have studied its complex ridge ribs and gullies, and I can see the resemblance. A sickle-shaped rock glacier pours out of a steep amphitheatre below the summit of the centre peak. Standing 1,500 metres above the level of the lake, this peak fills the sky opposite Atlin and dominates the lives and prospects of the townspeople.

We followed the trail, which was cut some years ago by students of the Glaciological Institute, along the foot of the mountain. Now overgrown, it meanders here and there, as game trails do. Beside a narrow lake, swathed in early morning mist, we came upon a moose drinking. Startled, it plunged into dense forest.

"Why do you keep kicking bear shit off the path?" asked Lucy, who had noticed my unsubtle attempts to prevent the children from seeing the steaming fresh evidence of a bear.

We scrambled over dead fall and through willow scrub to reach the toe of the rock glacier. Adam led the way up the steep, loose rock. Fallen from the frost-shattered headwalls of the cirque, this avalanche debris covers an icy bed that flows at a rate of one to two metres a year at its head and only a few millimetres a year at its toe (where the underlying ice becomes compressed). Radio-carbon dating of vegetation found buried in the depths shows it to be at least 8,000 years old. Although several rock glaciers exist in this region, the Atlin Mountain glacier is one of the most active.

From afar, the rock glacier looks like smooth scree, but up close it is an unstable field of constantly moving boulders. We followed a gully on the right-hand side scoured clean of loose rock by spring run-off. The scant vegetation offered good handholds. After two hours of climbing, the angle eased, and we entered a bowl with near-vertical walls.

We were tempted to follow a rocky spine that projected from the middle of the snow slope, but the rock was quite rotten and liable to bombard the person below with fragments. So Adam moved out onto the steep snow of the gully. When we hit a patch of ice, Judith protested, but, being tied in the middle of the rope, she had no choice but to continue. Trying to reverse and climb down would be even more scary.

We emerged into an alpine meadow below the summit cone of the mountain. Soft grass grew beside a stream where we slaked our thirst. The final glaciated pyramid faces north and is snow-covered throughout the year. In the distance, an anxious mother caribou encouraged her gangly calf across the steep snow. Fifty metres below the summit, we sheltered under an overhang. Adam lit a small camping stove, Judith made lunch, and Lucy melted snow for a drink of tea.

From the summit, we looked over the lakes of the southern Yukon and northwestern British Columbia and across the coastal mountain range to Mount Fairweather, which towers over Glacier Bay. Below us, we could plot our sailing passages among the pattern of islands at the south end of Atlin Lake.

As we started to descend, I remembered a previous expedition when a friend and I reached the summit in cloud that obscured our downward route. Able only to see a few yards ahead, we kept overcorrecting slightly to our right instead of trusting our compass. Once below the mist, we discovered that we were following a humpback ridge down the western side of the mountain diametrically opposite where we wished to be. The mist had crept farther down the mountain, and we were reluctant to climb back into it. So we spent a miserable eight hours battling ground willow and alder and eventually hit dense vegetation and dead fall timbers beside Torres Channel. We reached the boat exhausted. My friend promptly fell asleep in the cabin, and I was left to sail single-handedly across the lake in a rising gale. My climbing rope, which was lying on the deck, slowly slithered overboard out of my reach because I could not leave the tiller.

But on this occasion, the sun shone and the children were ex-ulted by their achievement in climbing the mountain in four hours. We descended a gully, taking care not to twist our ankles on the loose boulders. At the bottom, we plunged our faces into a stream of crystal water. From a shoulder of the southern peak of Atlin Mountain, a long scree chute of loose rock led down to the boat. Wearing leather work gloves, we grasped saplings and swung ape-like from bush to bush down the steep hillside towards *Ven*, which lay hidden in the bay behind a stand of spruce trees.

Above us, a snow-filled, sickle-shaped gully descended steeply from the south peak. Wayne Merry and I had climbed it the pre-vious spring by kicking the front points of our crampons into the firm crust and using our ice-axes for handholds in the snow. At the top, the wind had made an overhanging cornice through which we cut a hole and climbed out onto the summit.

One August day, Doug Lemond, a hunting guide, and I hiked into the high country on the back side of Atlin Mountain, where gentle hills cradle high alpine lakes. Our aim was to repair a small plywood hunting cabin that the porcupines had chewed.

I sailed across the lake to Torres Channel, where Doug was stay-ing with his mother-in-law, Boo Currelly. He spied me rounding the point and came down to the beach to help moor *Ven* to the dock. She lay next to his sleek black Indian canoe, the prow of which was fashioned in the traditional shape of a wolf's head — nose sniffing out the way ahead and ears cocked listening for any noise across the water.

Doug had researched drawings of Indian canoes used for whal-ing off Vancouver Island's west coast. He designed a hull ten me-tres long and two metres abeam with a bow suitable to throw off spray from big waves. He built the boat from plywood templates, using thin cedar strips laid in three layers at right angles to each other and sealed with epoxy resin. With the help of a five horse-power outboard motor, his canoe slips smoothly through the water. The four thwart seats, carrying up to eight persons, are lashed in place with thongs to make the hull flexible.

Doug peered out through thick glasses, which kept slipping down his nose, causing him to repeatedly push them back with his finger. Raising his eyebrows and furrowing his brow gave him a quizzical look of constant surprise. He had the rough, weathered hands of an outdoors man. A casual dresser, he wore jeans, a wool tartan shirt, and a loose windbreaker. His peaked cap, with its bobble on top, had fold-down ear pieces.

Doug used packhorses to carry gear to his mountain hunting camps at Sandy Lake, Rupert Lake, and Sheep Camp. Tack and pack gear hung under the eaves on the back wall of the cabin, where he also stored a chain-saw, axes, shovel, and other items for making bush life comfortable. He staked his horses under the trees close enough to the house to give warning of bears or wolves.

We saddled Doug's mountain pony Blazer, loaded some metal sheeting to patch the porcupine holes in the hut, and sauntered off carrying only small day packs. It felt good not to be encumbered by the heavy loads that are usually my lot when travelling in mountains. It reminded me of crossing the Bhutan Himalaya on a family journey in 1967, when we had ponies for Sarah and the children and carried no loads ourselves. For the first hour, we skirted the shore of Torres Channel, where Doug had cut a trail through dead fall timber. After crossing a creek by way of two fallen trunks, we began to climb along open escarpment. Rushing water in Plateau Creek resounded below to our left.

The trail climbed steeply through dense forest of spruce and balsam, where blisters on the bark oozed pungent, gelatinous gum. Steaming bear scats, laced with bright undigested berries, lay on the trail. The woods smelled sweetly after the recent rain, and the forest was quiet. I followed in Blazer's hoof prints while Doug, his felt hat with a horsehair band tilted on the back of his head, walked ahead holding the halter shank. We relished what Geoffrey Winthrop Young, author of *Mountaincraft*, calls "that silence which is the fellowship of the hills."

As we approached the alpine tundra, the woods thinned and we emerged into a meadow where a small stream flowed. We sat for a while, ate a tin of smoked oysters, drank cool water, and talked. Doug was brought up in Montana and wrangled horses as a boy. At the age of fourteen, he bought a pair of boots and a climbing rope and hiked into the Rockies. Later, he became a climbing guide and a ski patroller. He came to Canada to avoid being drafted to Vietnam, so he could not return home to the United States for fear of being imprisoned. First, he settled in southwestern Alberta, where he worked on a Stoney Indian reserve as director of a wilderness centre that taught traditional skills to native children. But the crowds surging into Banff Park drove him north to Atlin.

Doug bought the guiding and outfitting rights to a parcel of land half the size of Switzerland behind Atlin Mountain. It was encompassed by two arms of Tagish Lake: Graham Inlet to the north, and Taku Arm to the west. European and American clients would come on a ten-day hunt, which cost them between eight and ten thousand dollars, in order to kill an animal to hang in their trophy rooms back home in Munich or Houston. After they had shot "their" prize they would often quit the hunt and fly back home rather than rough it any longer in the inclement outdoors. Doug was tiring of this type of work that he fundamentally disapproved of, and soon after our hike he sold the hunting outfit.

Our conversation was curtailed by abundant mosquitoes and black flies that emerged from the meadows of burgeoning alpine flowers. In the space of a kilometre, I collected thirty different types of flowers. Our path led through a defile between two rocky mountains, where dwarf fireweed bordered several small lakes. The meadows were carpeted with lupins. The diversity of flower species recalled one springtime when I skied the Haute Route across the Swiss Alps.

After five hours of steady hiking, we reached Sheep Hut set on a rocky bluff. The walls and door of the plywood box, with its sloping roof, were well-chewed by porcupines, which relish the glue that binds plywood. We watched the sun set behind the peaks of Section Mountain, which dominates the south end of Torres Channel. Far below was densely-forested Section Creek, an unappealing route down.

We stoked the Yukon stove with resinous, aromatic balsam logs and brewed tea. While waiting for caribou steaks to cook, we scanned the hillsides with binoculars and a spotting scope, and Doug, familiar with the haunts and habits of game animals, spied a line of Stone Sheep crossing a high rocky scree in the far distance. Their huge curls of horns and their stony-grey coats distinguish them from the white-fleeced Dall Sheep.

Cosy in our sleeping bags, we listened to the gusts of wind that threatened to lift off the roof of the hut. We reminisced over less pleasant mountain bivouacs in former days when we were bold and indifferent to discomfort.

Then our conversation turned to Lillian Alling, a short, slender New Yorker who has become a legend in Atlin and a yardstick for toughness. Becoming homesick for her native Russia, she decided to cross the Bering Sea to Siberia. In September 1928, she passed through Atlin, stopping only long enough to buy a new pair of boots. She appeared outwardly reserved, especially in the presence of men, and was evasive about herself and her destination. On the Telegraph Trail, a lineman had turned her back; she was charged with vagrancy by the RCMP and was sent to Okalla Prison in Vancouver for three months.

Later, she returned and, accompanied by a pack-dog that drowned crossing a river, followed the Telegraph Trail to Atlin. From there, she set off for the Klondike dressed in tattered denim and wearing a different-sized man's boot on each foot. Sleeping out in the open, she took thirty-nine days to reach Dawson City, where the police promptly arrested her again. She got a job in a hostel for the winter, and the following spring she took a boat from Dawson to Eagle, Alaska. She eventually reached Nome, where she hired an Inuit to pilot her across the fifty-kilometre-wide Bering Strait to Russian soil. What became of her after that, nobody knows.

Next morning, we repaired the hut with sheet metal, left it shipshape, and descended by the same path we had climbed. On the way, we met a small herd of caribou and saw scats of bears in whose territory we had trespassed. We did not see the bears themselves, but we knew they were watching us from the forest.

Scotia Bay

Boating has been an important part of our life in Atlin, as indeed it has throughout the history of the town. A favourite family excursion was to sail from Atlin five kilometres across the lake to Scotia Bay to tread its historic ground and to visit our friends the Johnsons. They lived on a high bank halfway down the Atlinto River. One day, our family crew navigated *Ven* cautiously through the reefs and islands that lie offshore of the river, and headed towards a dome-shaped rock that stands guard at its mouth. White ripples warn of a sixty-metre gradient that creates hazardous waves and eddies over the four-kilometre length of the river. We tied *Ven* to one of the rotting pilings of the old dock, all that remains of the once-thriving Atlin Short Line Railway terminus, and dropped anchor astern to stop her from swinging with the wind.

Setting out towards the Johnson homestead, we walked along the disused railway track that runs parallel to the beach for a hundred metres and then disappears into the trees. Most of the century-old rails and ties have long since gone, but a few rusty spikes lie scattered among the lupins and rose bushes beside the sandy track.

We heard a commotion of dogs from down the track, and then Bruce Johnson came into view. Like Jehu in his chariot, he was standing in his summer training jalopy, made from the bones of a

Volkswagen chassis stripped of everything except the steering wheel and brake pedal. His black curly beard framed a rugged face and, by habit, he nibbled his moustache with his lower teeth. In response to his order, the team of ten dogs came to a halt and crouched obediently in traces attached to the front axle.

"Hi! Are you folks coming for a visit?" Bruce boomed. "I'm going to the dock to collect some freight from my canoe. I'll be back soon. Go ahead and ask Jeaniel to make tea."

On the command "okay," the team , a motley confusion of yelping dogs with muzzles forward and ears laid back, took off like the wind.

The Johnson homestead lay halfway along the old railway track. A sign read: "No hunting — kids playing." Bruce's other dogs, eighteen in all, were each secured on a short chain. They sat atop their individual kennels and howled in concert — a wail that echoed from the surrounding hills. Our children were nervous about running the gauntlet of yapping dogs until Bruce's wife, Jeaniel, came out and quieted them. We gave her Bruce's message and proposed that we would walk on to Taku Landing at the end of the track and visit with them on our way back.

Another two kilometres farther on, we left the woods and, through some aspen trees, could see the last white water rapid of the Atlinto River emptying into Graham Inlet. In an open area ahead stood Taku Landing, a handsome wood building that was once the terminal for boats coming up Tagish Lake from Carcross.

The station waiting room was panelled with tongue-and-groove fir. A long bench stood beside the guichet, where some old tickets lay — mementos of more than half a century before. In those days, especially at the height of the tourist season, Taku was a busy port. A platform allowed rail cars to roll alongside the boat's loading bay. Some old pier supports had collapsed and the last few flat cars were about to slip backwards into the water.

Judith, Sarah
and Lucy with
Bruce Johnson's
buggy, used for
training racing
dogs during the
summer.

In the nearby locomotive shed, gooey patches of oil spattered
the floor around an inspection pit, and rusty ironware lay on work-
benches from which the tools had long since disappeared. Hidden
in willow saplings on a bank above the track stood the railway men's
quarters and a bunkhouse cabin. A midden of jettisoned rusty cans
and chipped enamel cooking pots lay in the undergrowth beside
the tilting skeleton of an old outhouse.

In 1898, a wagon road was built across the isthmus between
Taku Landing and Scotia Bay. This was soon replaced by a pine pole
railroad, upon which a cart, set on two pairs of railroad wheels, was
pulled by a horse. Before proper carriages were built, passengers sat
on their own baggage and had to get out to help push the cart when
the grade was too steep. Shortly thereafter, the definitive Atlin Short
Line Railway, also known as the Atlin Southern, was built. A nar-
row-gauge locomotive, the *Duchess*, built in 1878, was bought from
the Dunsmuir coal mines near Nanaimo on Vancouver Island,
shipped to Skagway, and taken by scow to Taku. It served that area

well for many years and now stands on display outside the Caribou Hotel in Carcross. Because there were no turntables, the engine did a push-me-pull-you up the line and back.

Eventually, the Taku Tramway rolling stock comprised six flat cars for freight, a caboose, and one passenger carriage for forty-eight people. The latter had open sides and pull-blinds to keep out the sparks and the sun. Swallows built their nests under the car eaves and flew along beside the train to keep watch on their young. The two dollars each way passenger fare — at fifty cents a mile — made it the most expensive rail journey in Canada.

When the White Pass & Yukon Route bought the Atlin Short Line Railway, it assured its monopoly of transport in the region. The company blamed the steep charges on the cost of buying and shipping engines and rolling stock, multiple-handling fees, and a short navigation season on the lakes. These excuses are all still used today to account for the excessive cost of goods and transport in the North. The White Pass & Yukon Route stranglehold was broken in the 1930s when airplanes began to service Atlin. At this time, the company closed down their operation on Atlin Lake.

To savour the history of Taku, I cast my mind back more than half a century. Out of the wilderness the *S. S. Tutshi* heaves in sight as it chugs up the middle of Graham Inlet, which extends west between the steep enclosing arms of Atlin Mountain and Table Mountain. Smoke rises from its tall yellow stack, and a steam whistle hoots. An orange paddle-wheel astern churns the water into white froth. At its masthead flies the Canadian Red Ensign and the pennant of the British Yukon Navigation Company.

Eager passengers lean on the rail of the upper deck. They spot a flock of mountain sheep, white dots that dance across Table Mountain's rocky bluffs and south-facing slopes. The crew prepare hawsers for docking and the captain in the wheel house manoeuvers the ship against a pier of huge pile-driven logs. The little train backs along the line into position so that passengers have to walk only a few steps to their carriage and freight can be unloaded directly onto

The Duchess and open passenger car 232 on the Atlin tramway in the 1920s. *(Canadian Pacific Limited, 4103)*

flat cars. Ladies wearing bonnets, blouses with leg-of-mutton sleeves, and long skirts and men in knickerbockers and trilby hats wander around the little community. A whistle blows to warn of the train's imminent departure. Passengers climb into the open-sided carriage, and the *Duchess* gets up steam and puffs out along the track towards Scotia Bay. There, it will meet the steamer *Tarahne*, which will carry the passengers across the lake to Atlin.

Coming back to the present from our look back into the past, we set off back to the Johnson's cabin on a narrow path that left the railway track and hugged the crest of the river bank. Small piles of moose droppings littered the path. The current was fast and formed standing waves where it rushed past big boulders. It cut into the bank, exposing layers of pebbles. Skilled motor boatmen can run up and down the river, but there is always a danger of a propeller being torn off on a submerged rock.

The Johnson's cabin stood in a forest clearing. By dint of many additions, it had become a two-storey house. An assortment of racing harnesses and dog traces hung on a wall of an ample porch. A large wood stove occupied the centre of the living room, off of which were the family bedrooms. A log cabin for guests stood near the river bank.

Jeaniel gave us a vivacious welcome, and soon Bruce's dogs announced their master's return. Sarah and I sat at a big scrubbed kitchen table and drank tea while the Johnson children took ours off to explore the yard. Seeing the Johnson family living in the bush close to the land made us aware of the wilderness we were privileged to share. Even though our family was more focused on the city, at least we could retreat to our cabin in Atlin where we could savour the bush life that we could not lead ourselves.

"Bruce and I met in Alaska at the University of Fairbanks," said Jeaniel. "We were both studying biology. When we got married, we worked as weather observers at Macmillan Pass. It was mighty remote up there at the end of the North Canol Road. We were right on the Northwest Territories border. We dabbled in trapping and driving dogs, and Bruce entered some races."

Bruce's skill and success increased, and he went on to become a champion musher. Six times, he won the 210-mile Percy deWolfe race from Dawson City to Fortymile and back. He competed in the Alaska Iditarod race between Anchorage and Nome. Then, in 1986, he won the Yukon Quest, a thousand-mile race between Fairbanks and Whitehorse — the first Yukoner ever to do so. This was the most prestigious win of his entire racing career.

Bruce's racing dogs were bred more for stamina than looks. His team was an ill-assorted, but speedy, bunch of mongrels. His dogs' offspring are now spread throughout kennels in the Yukon and Alaska.

"In the early days, I picked out a yellow Labrador-husky cross as a likely lead dog," said Bruce, taking up the story. "We named him Thor. He was pulling in the traces at six months old. Even though he was poorly built for a racing dog, he went on to win fourteen out of seventeen consecutive races." Thor was obedient to a fault, always willing to please, and docile with the children. He had unlimited drive when it came to racing and an instinctive sense of direction; even when out on the lake at night in a blizzard, he could find the start of a portage. He served as the guardian of the Johnson homestead, using different barks to warn of moose, fox, wolf, bear, and humans.

"One evening, I was alerted by his 'person' bark,'" said Jeaniel. "I went down to the river to see what the fuss was about. Across the river was an Atlin man, frost-bitten and hypothermic. His cries for helped were drowned by the roar of the water. I called for help, and Bruce came. He got the boat started and brought him over."

Then one dark night wolves got into Thor's kennel and dragged him off, abruptly terminating his long life and distinguished racing career.

In November 1993, Bruce Johnson went out on Little Atlin Lake to train for the Yukon Quest. He and a team of eight dogs left from his cabin off the Tagish Road, where the family had spent several winters to avoid the inconvenience and the dangers of crossing the lake in spring and fall. It was his second run of the day, and the temperature had dropped to minus 34 degrees Celsius. His son-in-law Tim Buerge, who lived in a neighbouring cabin, saw Bruce mushing down his training trail towards the lake. When he had not returned by seven in the evening, Tim harnessed another dog team and went to investigate. He followed Bruce's tracks along the edge of the lake ice for about ten kilometres. Then they turned around and returned by the same route. The tracks were quite close to the lake edge, where the ice is thickest, and Bruce had evidently tested it with his axe in several places.

Halfway along the crescentic trail, Bruce's dogs had suddenly headed off at right angles towards the centre of the lake. Tim followed cautiously; he knew that this part of the lake had not yet frozen over. In the dark, he could just discern the tracks going towards an open lead of water. It was too dangerous to proceed, so Tim returned home to summon help. With some RCMP divers, he returned to search for Bruce at first light. They could see dog sled tracks leading straight to the edge of open water. Then they disappeared. There were no signs of Bruce having applied his sled brakes and no signs of struggle at the edge of the broken ice. The divers found, ten metres down, Bruce's body slumped behind his sled along with the dogs. His head lamp was in the sled bag and not on his head, as might be expected, and his knife was still in its sheath. Bruce had gone through the ice before and knew the techniques for trying to extricate himself.

The mystery of Bruce's death remains unsolved. He was too experienced a musher to have lost control of his team. If the dogs had headed out into the centre of the lake, which Bruce knew not to be properly frozen, he would have applied his brake. If that had failed, he would have jumped off the sled when the first dogs went through the ice. Some months before, Bruce had hit his head when he had collided with a tree on a training run. Some catastrophic event in his brain, like a haemorrhage, would have shown up on post mortem examination; but it did not. We may never know what happened that fateful night. What is certain is that Bruce's family, his friends, and the dog-mushing world lost a Titan.

After our visit with the Johnsons, we sailed back to Atlin and tied *Ven* up to the dock on Front Street opposite the site of the old White Pass Hotel. Nearby, on the foreshore along Front Street, some of Atlin's historic boats are beached. Since the turn of the century, many sturdy craft have sailed on Atlin Lake, and some have got into trouble from its violent and rapid changes of weather. The sight of their hulks brings their stories to mind .

Atlin's boating history started indirectly in 1898, when Captain John Irving founded the Irving Navigation Company on Lake Bennett. Many boats were built there to transport stampeders to the

The White Pass Hotel and boats along Atlin's waterfront. *(Yukon Archives/Atlin Historical Society Collection, p. 106)*

Klondike gold fields. Irving bought the *Scotia* in Seattle, shipped her in pieces to Carcross, and hauled them over the ice to Scotia Bay, where shipwrights assembled them. After 20 years of service, this work horse was retired because she was hard to handle in strong winds and violent mountain down draughts. She was succeeded by the *M. V. Tarahne*, which is now cradled in a timber ship way across from the Atlin Inn.

The *Tarahne* was designed by the navigation company's marine architect A. E. Henderson, who was responsible for building several other famous steamboats that plied the Yukon river systems — the *Tutshi,* the *Casca,* the *Nasutlin,* and the *Keno.* When the *Tarahne* was being built, Taku Jack, the local Indian chief, suggested calling her Tey-a-ha-hin-ee, which means "a mountain creek running over flat rocks." White men couldn't pronounce that euphonic name, however, so the boat was named *Tarahne.*

Originally 30 metres long, the *Tarahne* was sawn in half in 1928 and lengthened to carry more tourists. In a typical season, she made as many as 130 voyages between Scotia Bay and Atlin. Loaded with freight and nearly 200 passengers, she cruised at 12 knots. She also ran tourist trips around Teresa Island. Like her predecessor *Scotia*, she docked at Scotia Bay at the end of the Taku Tram railway. Being the source of the Atlinto River, the bay always had open water, and it was protected from winter storms and crunching spring ice by many small offshore islands. During the winter, the *Tarahne* was left to freeze into the ice at Safety Cove, north of Scotia Bay; it was better for her timbers than letting them dry out on the ship ways on shore.

A White Pass & Yukon Route company report noted that "The *Tarahne* is a very fine rough-weather boat, and no trouble was experienced while she was working this season." Less than ten years after she was lengthened and re-fitted, the *Tarahne* was put out of service because of the depression, which strangled the tourist trade. She was laid up on ways on the Atlin foreshore in 1936, never to sail again.

Alongside the *Tarahne* lies the sleek pleasure cruiser *Atlinto*. Jules Eggert built her in his spare time with the help of local men. He skippered a midnight cruise that left Atlin at 10 p.m. and arrived at the head of the Llewellyn Inlet at midnight. From there, tourists could hike a trail to the snout of the Llewellyn Glacier.

The low hulk of the *S. S. Gladys,* beached in front of the Glaciological Institute, looks sad lying tilted to one side; her planks are rotting and her cabin and wheel house are derelict. She once ran the mail and tugged barges across from Scotia Bay to the White Pass dock that stood in front of the hotel.

The White Pass Hotel was built in 1916 to handle the growing tourist traffic that spun off from the Skagway-Whitehorse railway. It was a magnificent construction for so small a town; it had three wings, each three stories high, projecting from a main axis. One annual company report states that "We now have the finest hotel in the North Country." Arriving guests disembarked from the

Tarahne at the hotel dock and walked a short way to the reception desk to be welcomed by summer staff (local women and university students). The hotel offered tourist boat trips down the lake, fishing, hiking, and golf on a course near the Pine Creek bridge. Another attraction at the north end of town was the mineral spring. The water here was cold, slightly effervescent from carbonates, and laxative due to magnesia. The White Pass & Yukon Route built a gazebo there that still stands today, albeit heeling askew.

The tourism slump of the 1930s that had caused the retirement of the *Tarahne* also resulted in the demise of the White Pass Hotel. One wing was dismantled and rebuilt at the north end of town where it became the Atlin Hospital. Staffed by a doctor and two nurses, it closed after a year, but was re-opened in 1954 as a Red Cross outpost hospital. Ten years later, the University of Michigan took over the building, now called the Glaciological Institute, as a base for its Juneau Ice Field Research Program.

Talking of transport and the old White Pass Hotel brings us to Atlin's early cars. Count E. J. de Lamarre, explorer, president of the French Automobile Club, member of the French Academy of Sciences, and editor of the *Klondike Review of Paris,* drove the first car into town. He arrived in Skagway with a 1900 model five horsepower automobile and a three-wheeler auto cycle, both flying the French flag. De Lamarre and his companion took the train to Bennett and set out across lake ice towards Atlin as part of a 20,000-kilometre publicity tour for the French newspaper *Le Figaro.* His private secretary travelled behind in a horse-drawn sleigh carrying extra gasoline and spares. They broke down many times on the way, lost various parts, and once had to cut a hole in the ice to get at the sump burner that was submerged in overflow.

The Count bought hydraulic mining leases on Boulder Creek and stayed on in Atlin. He had champagne shipped regularly from France to bolster his aristocratic lifestyle, but he lost 40 cases to Atlin's first major fire. The loss was valued at $1,200 — a small fortune at the time. After the fire, the count bought several claims in the Klondike and disappeared thither.

Soon, many well-known makes of car appeared in Atlin. Bill Roxborough, proprietor of the Kootenay Hotel, ran tourists out to the gold creeks and to Ruffner's silver mine in one of his two McLaughlin-Buicks and a nine-passenger Studebaker with plush purple upholstery and a roll-back top. Louis Schulz also owned Buicks and a Cadillac that carried a compressor for pumping flat tires. Cyril James, Frank Henning, and Ross Peebler were drivers of the several makes of car — Model T Ford, Straight-8 Hudson, and Nash Oldsmobile — that were parked outside the hotel waiting to take tourists up the creeks where they might try their hand at gold panning.

Marco Pini was one miner who advertised panning on his claim and encouraged business by salting the dirt with a few flakes of gold. When the tourists found gold, they would often tip him generously and brag to their friends back at the hotel. Interested, other tourist would come to Pini to try their luck at panning.

One day, Pini hitched a ride to town in a car filled with tourists. The trip was a long one because of the bad road and the two lady passengers who repeatedly asked the driver to drop them off so they could "pick some flowers." The driver would move a discreet distance down the road while the ladies disappeared into the bush. During the journey, they repeated their request twice more.

Pini, himself getting uncomfortable, eventually piped up. "Driver, I wanna go picka da daisy."

"Marco, we're almost in town," said the driver. "You'll just have to wait."

A mile or so further, Pini repeated his request and received the same refusal.

"Driver, if you donna stoppa da car," shouted Pini, "I'm gonna picka da daisy right on da back seat."

Ben-my-Chree

One July, Doug Lemond took Sarah, Lucy, and me on an expedition to Ben-my-Chree, a tiny settlement surrounded by mountains at the very head of the Taku Arm of Tagish Lake. We went on the plywood river boat that he had built the previous winter. Painted red, the flat-bottomed, wooden-ribbed boat was six metres long. The squared bow was decked and steep-angled to throw waves clear of the boat.

Doug operated the outboard motor from the stern. We sat in the bottom of the boat on large canvas kit bags packed with sleeping bags, clothes, and camping gear. Waterproof storage boxes held the food; other gear was stowed in flotation chambers under the thwarts.

The mouth of the Atlinto River flowed swiftly with mountain melt water. Nearby stood a casting platform for fly-fishermen. Halfway down the river, Bruce Johnson's dogs became aware of us and set up a plaintive howl. Doug navigated the turbulent river, avoiding some large boulders, and emerged into the quiet water of Graham Inlet beside Taku Landing. In a bay on the south side of the inlet, we explored some old cabins on the site of an abandoned sawmill. We saw piles of rotten lumber slabs and cordwood that had been cut a century ago.

With his telescope, Doug spotted mountain sheep on the cliffs of Table Mountain. Before reaching Golden Gate, we visited Brooklands, a log homestead where the Brook family has lived for three generations. A huge dining table serves the extended family of Marion, Reg Brook Junior's widow, who runs a bed and breakfast. Summer visitors stay in the guest cabins, and Wisconsin University geology students annually make it their base camp for field trips into the mountains around Ben-my-Chree. Marion's son Jim traps in winter and has a summer fish camp and a commercial flying business. Pilots of small planes flying to or from Whitehorse often drop by for a cup of tea and a chat. In this wild place, the Brooks' most isolated time is the couple of months at spring break-up and fall freeze-up when the ice is too dangerous for Jim's plane to take off.

Reginald Brook Senior arrived at Engineer Mine to join his old school chum Captain James Alexander, who had bought a major interest in the mine some years before. Reg had been six years old when he met Alexander at boarding school in England, and they became lifelong friends. The British have a bizarre custom of farming out their young children to private schools. Many boys were packed off to the dominions or the colonies after their schools had made men of them.

When they were both sixteen, the friends parted, and Alexander went to London to study medicine. In 1898, after only two years, he gave up his studies and left for British Columbia; Reg Brook followed. They bought a half interest in a ten-ton schooner to prospect along the British Columbia coast.

Two years later, Alexander left for England to enlist in the Boer War. By saying he was five years older than he was, he was able to join the Rough Riders as galloper (courier) to the Commander-in-Chief. Later, he became a captain in the 3rd Dragoon Guards. After the war, he returned to Vancouver, moved north, and hunted and prospected in the Atlin area.

In 1908, he staked an abandoned property west of Atlin Mountain on the shore of Taku Arm — Engineer Mine. He had two partners in this venture: Allan Smith, a businessman from Philadelphia who had arrived in Atlin by dog sled with his hunting guide via the Telegraph Trail, and Jack Pilling, who had packed in a pedal organ. "Cap" Alexander appointed his old friend Reg Brook as manager of the mine and of the Wann River hydroelectric project that provided power for the mine.

The Brook family subsequently moved from the mine to their present homestead at the mouth of Rupert Creek, which Reg Brook acquired after the tragic death of the former resident. One September evening Taku Jim's son saw Red Rupert, a trapper, paddling his canoe near Golden Gate. During the night, there arose an extremely heavy south wind. Captain McDonald, skipper of the *S.S. Tutshi* reported that his ship had almost been blown ashore. He stated that he had never experienced a storm like that in his entire career. Rupert was not seen again, but the wreckage of his canoe and a paddle were found next day by Reg Brook, who went to Atlin to report the tragedy to the provincial constable.

On his trips between Engineer Mine and Atlin, Reg Brook had frequently stayed at the cabin of Red Rupert, who had squatted there without title. So when Rupert died, Reg Senior bought the cabin from the Gold Commissioner and had 40 surrounding acres surveyed for a Crown Grant. At the foot of a seventy-foot waterfall upstream, moose often visited a grayling pool, and trout thrived in the crystal clear water of Rupert Creek. This Eden became the family home of Reg, whose favourite saying was, "You live with the land up here; don't force it." Reg Brook Junior also settled on the property and made annual spring visits to Whitehorse to buy groceries and to deliver pelts to the fur auctions.

We left Brooklands and set off towards Golden Gate, a crossroads where Graham Inlet joins the Taku Arm of Tagish Lake. Wind howled out of the south, and white foam blew off the crests of choppy waves, yet the boat was stable and shipped little water as Doug quartered into the wind.

The ghost town of Engineer was nestled between Bee Peak and Gleaner Mountain. To the west lies the entry portal to Atlin from the White Pass via Fantail Lake. Nearby is Bighorn Creek, which was named by Fred Lawson, an old-timer who, in 1876, at the age of sixteen, was a mule boy in Colonel George Custer's force that was sent to subdue the Sioux Indians in Montana. Lawson was sent back with the mules to rejoin the main column when the battle of Little Bighorn began. He was one of the few survivors of the Last Stand. Custer and over 200 of his men were slaughtered one by one after being surrounded on a hilltop by Indians. Another version tells of Custer being smothered to death by a squaw who sat on his head.

Landing at Engineer Mine, we hauled the boat up the beach using some logs laid out as rollers. Close to shore stood the derelict mill, built against the side of the mountain. Hard rock, brought from underground workings in rail car trolleys, was tipped straight into the top of a giant sieve. Small rock fell into a jaw crusher that reduced it to pieces of less than five centimetres in diameter. These pieces then fell into a gyratory cone crusher and onto to a ball mill where it was ground by huge steel ball-bearings. The crushed rock was then treated with pyrite, cyanide, and mercury amalgam. Any floating residue went to the floater plant. Using air suction, gold concentrate, which had settled on a canvas drum, was dried and finally scraped off.

On the surrounding hillsides lay many old buildings, ghosts of an era past. The sight of some modern machinery indicated to us that miners were still busy at Engineer hoping to find the riches promised by early prospectors.

Engineer Mine has a tangled history. In 1900, the American chief engineer in charge of construction of the White Pass & Yukon Railway decided to prospect the interior coastal region opened up by the railroad. He grubstaked a small party of his assistants to stake ground on the east shore of Tagish Lake and they named it Engineer Mine. Next year, with the railway completed, the chief engineer took a party of men to the mine to do the assessment work required by law. This completed, he went to Atlin to record the work, put his claims in order, and register his syndicate as the Aga Gold Mining Co. Ltd. Not being familiar with mining procedures, he asked for help and was directed to "Cap" Alexander, who was well known in the Atlin mining circles.

Apparently, the company made several mistakes. It failed to get a Free Miner's Certificate, which was required by British Columbian law to own any sort of mineral claim or mining property; without such a certificate, a property was not legally titled. Mr. Edward Bourne, the company secretary, re-located the claims and signed a false affidavit to say that the obligatory assessment work had been done. Alexander suggested that Bourne add the expenses of his trip from Seattle to his assessment work expenses, which he did. With this information Alexander tried to blackmail Bourne to drop his claims and quit the country. When Bourne resisted, Alexander reported him to the Atlin police. Bourne was arrested and was jailed for swearing a false oath. When released, he promptly fled back to the United States. Alexander waited for the lease on the ground to expire and then staked all the holdings for himself.

One of the partners in the Chief Engineer's original syndicate, a lawyer from Skagway, on hearing of the business with Alexander, put a solemn curse on the property. He prophesied that "Nothing but death and disaster would be the lot of anyone associated with Engineer Mine."

Alexander went ahead regardless and mined successfully for several summers. Each winter, he took his gold to Vancouver to deposit it and then he went out to paint the town red. Rumours spread about the fabulous Engineer Mine and its notorious owner.

Early on, a few strange events occurred, possibly attributable to the lawyer's curse. In the spring of 1912, Stanley McLennan, who had been working some claims at Engineer, moved to Ben-my-Chree. A round of charges, fired in a tunnel, set off a snow slide that swept through the cookhouse where McLennan and his wife were peeling potatoes. When their bodies were dug out, one held a potato and the other a paring knife.

Shortly afterwards, Jimmie Stewart, an assayer at Engineer, went crazy while recovering from a drinking toot. He downed a beaker of potassium cyanide mixed with nitric acid — his last cocktail.

Three years later, a Yugoslav miner was blown up after drilling into an abandoned hole still filled with gunpowder when he was sinking a winze shaft in 'E' vein. Then, in 1918, a Japanese cook, who was new to the mine, fell out with the steam engineer, slashed at his own throat and then killed himself by hara-kiri. He was taken to the doctor in Atlin, but died following some primitive surgery.

The death toll was already up to four when, on October 23, 1918, Alexander, his wife, and two engineers, who were interested in taking an option for the Mining Corporation of Canada, took passage on the Canadian Pacific Railway Company's steamship *Princess Sophia*. There were 353 passengers and crew and five dogs on this last boat of the year heading south from Skagway.

Three hours after sailing, at about two in the morning on October 24th, at full speed, in pitch dark, and in a blinding snowstorm, the *Princess Sophia* struck Vanderbilt Reef in the middle of the Lynn Canal. Next morning, at the lowest ebb of the tide, she was perched three metres out of the water and surrounded by at least a dozen boats that had responded to the skipper's call for help.

The passengers could have been rescued by landing row-boats on the rock, but Captain Noble refused to allow it. He preferred to wait for his own company's vessel sent from Vancouver, over a thousand miles and many days away, rather than accept help from another boat that might claim the wreck as salvage.

The following night, a fierce northerly storm blew up and the rescue boats returned to shelter in Juneau harbour. The tide rose and lifted the *Princess Sophia* off the rock. She slid backwards off the reef and foundered with all souls. Alexander went down with two ore sacks full of his best high-grade gold. The only survivor was an English setter that later turned up at Auke Bay, near Juneau.

The Curse continued to take its toll. Alexander had willed his estate to his partner, Allan Smith. The original will was lost, so Smith could not claim his benefits. He cabled to Engineer Mine for Alexander's papers. Mailman Jack Fox was carrying five canvas bags of papers when he went through the ice near Golden Gate. The sack with the packages held air long enough to freeze into the ice; Jack Fox drowned. The papers were retrieved and forwarded to Smith, but they contained no original will. In April 1919, Smith shot himself through the heart. Shortly after, the original will was found in the private safe of the manager of the Bank of Montreal.

Nine people associated with Engineer Mine had died so far, and still the curse didn't let up. In 1922 one of the Engineer miners was drowned in a boating accident. Three years later, the mine superintendent developed cancer of the neck and died. Soon after, another mailman, travelling from Engineer to Ben-my-Chree, fell through the ice off Holyhead Point and froze to death. Later that year the superintendent's wife became ill and died. A young engineer sent to operate Engineer Mine by a crooked New York financier slipped and fell under the train that was to take him and his bride on the first leg of their journey north.

The disasters continued. In 1927, a miner who was hauling a heavy motor up a steep grade fell over and died. Soon after, one miner died in his boat near the mine, and another went to the lake for a bucket of water and, upon return, died in his cabin doorway. Around this time, a mining engineer, who was in the Philippines waiting to take up his appointment at Engineer, fell down a mine shaft and was killed.

We were all sobered by the thought of the curse that had wrought havoc with the small community. The wind having died, we launched the boat and, in the light of a low-slung sun, headed for the elbow of the Taku Arm at Holyhead Point, the last wag of the tail of Tagish Lake. There, the Wann River drains out of Edgar and Nelson Lakes and the low-lying neck of land that separates Tagish Lake from Atlin Lake.

At the mouth of the Wann River, we camped on a sandy shore that sloped to a protected crescent-shaped bay. There we tested our safety suits and were surprised to find that we were still comfortable after forty-five minutes floating immobile in the water. Sarah, Lucy, and I explored a path through the bush behind the camp and found the powerhouse of the old flume, formerly a conduit for the water mill that made hydro-electric power for Engineer Mine. Old buildings were overgrown with bush, boards had been ripped up, rafters were falling in, and old magazines papered the walls. I thought of the time when this place was busy with people — a time when machinery rolled noisily and abundant gold was being dug out of the ground.

From our Wann River camp, a short run due west brought us to Ben-my-Chree, where the Swanson River flows out of the mountains and disgorges into a braided delta between White Moose Mountain to the north and the Florence Range to the south.

We walked up the long wooden pier, which allowed boats to dock in the low water of spring and late summer. Ducking under some overgrown trees and bushes, we emerged into an open area where cosmos daisies and poppies surrounded the old homestead, a handsome house of weathered wood overtowered by jagged mountains. Through these mountains, we caught a glimpse of glaciers and snow peaks on the edge of the coastal range, one of the most remote places in the north. Situated at the end of a very long lake, Ben-my-Chree has wild water in front and green grass in the untended gardens behind.

In the 1930s, Otto Partridge and his wife built this homestead and cultivated a garden. Otto, or 'Swampy" as he was nicknamed, arrived in Skagway in 1897. Colonel Conrad of Windy Arm named him "The Swampfox," shortened to "Swampy," because "of all the foxes, the swampfox is the foxiest." Partridge hid $20,000 in a barrel of oakum designated for caulking ships' hulls, in order to bypass Soapy Smith's gang, which was terrorizing Skagway at that time.

Partridge started the Bennett Lake & Klondike Navigation Company and ran the boats *Ora, Flora* and *Nora* until he lost his business to the White Pass & Yukon Route. He bought the sawmill at Millhaven Bay off the West Arm of Lake Bennett near Carcross, and he and his wife and lived there on a houseboat. He explored the Southern Lakes in a home-built sailing yacht named Ben-my-Chree, which means "girl of my heart" in Manx, the ancient language of the Isle of Man, where he went to school.

Gold was found at the very end of Taku Arm, so the Partridges moved their houseboat there. They were accompanied by Miss Emily Dalton, who had come out from London to assist Bishop Bompas in his work in the Yukon. She became friends with the Partridges, settled down with them, and helped them develop the mine, along with Lord Egerton, an English aristocrat who pooled his money to join the venture.

Swampy often visited Engineer Mine for a chat with Cap Alexander, who used to say to him, "You can come to my cabin to talk, but none of that old family stuff." He was referring to Partridge's penchant, acquired through his proximity to Lord Egerton, for name-dropping and claiming aristocratic family connections.

"I asked old Swampy into my cabin one day," recounted Alexander. "He began talking and I fell asleep. He kept on talking to the missus and, do you know, the old rascal popped a couple of his brothers into the House of Lords while I slept."

Soon after they began mining, a rock and snow avalanche destroyed the aerial tramway and killed the caretakers. The mine was closed down and the effects were moved to Engineer. Undeterred, the Partridges moved ashore to the site of their dream house, Ben-my-Chree. They built cabins and greenhouses and laid out vegetable

and flower gardens where they grew sweet peas, delphiniums, as-
ters, columbines, peonies, and pansies.

In their comfortable log home, the Union Jack hung on the wall
beside the Stars and Stripes. A Japanese manservant poured tea for
guests, who were expected to sign the visitors' book and to leave
their visiting cards in a silver salver placed on top of the harmonium.
The Partridges persuaded the White Pass & Yukon Route to extend
the route of the *S. S. Tutshi* from Engineer Mine to Ben-my-Chree
so that tourists might stop for a drink of home-brewed rhubarb
wine and experience this northern showplace before going on to
Taku Landing and Atlin. The guest book of Ben-my-Chree contains the names of many distinguished tourists. Mrs. Partridge, an
aristocratic, old-fashioned woman, oversaw the establishment
which, day-by-day, was really run by Miss Emily Dalton. Otto Partridge entertained the guests. He died in 1930, followed within
months by his wife.

Our happy and interesting expedition to Engineer Mine and
Ben-my-Chree over, we started the motor and chugged back to
Taku Landing. There, Sarah, Lucy, and I disembarked and walked
along the tramway, while Doug ran the boat upstream against the
flow of the Atlinto River. We met him at Scotia Bay and were soon
back in the comfort of our cabin.

FALL

Bears, Salmon, and Eagles

Bears, salmon, and eagles are the North's most majestic creatures and hold a special place in our musings about summer and fall. Although I have had no close encounters with bears myself, whenever we are out hiking in the bush we are very aware of the danger of disturbing them.

"Always talk polite to a bear," said Solomon Charlie, an old Indian trapper. "If you meet him, say in a soft voice, 'Please go away, Mr. Bear'."

Joe Martin, a patient of mine, had lived in the bush all his life and had a wealth of bear stories. "Down that river there," Joe said, "we hunt beaver quite a few year ago. A grizzly bear, he run after me, so I shoot him. I kill that one. You see lots of them around there but, y'know, I don't want to shoot him if he don't bother me. Another one, I wave hello to him and I talk loud, 'Hey, Mr. Bear, you go that way and I go this way.' He do it, and he go away and don't bother me. Always talk nice to a bear. I don't kill animal for nothing. Only if I need meat. Always talk nice to a bear."

Joe used to come to my clinic just for the excuse of telling me a new story. "This Indian, he loved to eat bear meat, like you like pork chops, so he hunt bear all the time. He kill lots of bear and he skin the whole works. Then he climb inside the skin and he look like a real bear. He has no gun, but he has spear in his hand and he walk around and pretend he's a bear. He go out on the mountain to hunt bear and he have another man to watch him in case a bear get wind of him. He catch lots of bear meat and make big fire and throw in lots of bear fat. Real bear, he smell that burning fat right away because the wind blow towards him, and he come along and see another bear walking around there though it's really a man inside the bear skin with a spear in his hand. He wait for his good chance and pretty soon the bear he stand alongside him and the man he put his spear right through bear's heart."

"One time he make a mistake," said Joe. "Real bear, he jumped on top of man and he get mad and fight him and knock him down. Now the man who's there to watch him, he run and get another spear. When he got back he say to him, 'Which one? Top one or bottom?' 'Top one,' he said. The one on the top he's the real bear. The man he come along with the spear and he kill that bear."

"You're not supposed to talk about bear in winter time," Joe continued, "because he'll hear and come after you in spring and get smart with you. One day, Mrs. Bear she grab a man and get him to sleep with her all winter, and she let him go in springtime. 'Now promise not to tell your people where you been and what you done,' she say. But the Indians asked the man where he'd been all winter. He say nothing for a long time. Then finally he tell them where he was and where the bear den is. The Indians dressed the man up and coloured his face and went after the bear. 'We'll protect you,' they say and they put him in the middle of them and went off to find the bear hole. But the bear, she recognized the man, got smart with him, and killed him right there."

Joe was in full swing now. "This Indian, he had muzzle-loader and he go look for bear. Bear she come and the Indian he throw the gun away and climb spruce tree. Bear she take hold of the gun and point it at him, but she don't know how to pull the trigger with them long claws of hers. Bear go away at last and he come down from the tree. But he lost his muzzle-loader 'cuz bear she take it away to her cave."

The grizzly bear is a beast of uneven temper and immense size; an average adult male weighs about 300 kilograms and stands three metres tall on his hind legs. *Ursus arctos* is distinguished from other bears by its dish-shaped face and the prominent hump over the base of its neck. Its fur ranges in colour from rich brown to a blonde greyish "grizzled" tint. A powerful long-distance swimmer, the grizzly does a sort of dog-paddle. Long claws, used for digging roots and combing berry bushes, are unsuited to climbing trees, which the smaller black bear does with ease.

Grizzlies avoid humans by choice. But they may attack when frightened, disturbed during the mating season, or separated from their cubs or their food cache by an intruder. In summer, they usually feed on shoots, berries, roots, and ground squirrels, but when they find easy fodder in camps or garbage dumps they can become "spoiled" and scavenge human habitats. People are not their usual fare, and they eat meat only when they can't find other food. This happened during a smallpox outbreak in the last century on the Alaskan coast when bears developed taste for human flesh.

In the fall, bears eat huge quantities of berries to build up fat reserves for the winter. They don't actually hibernate, but they lie dormant in dens all winter and live off their stored fat. If awakened, they are extremely cantankerous.

Bears have acute senses of smell and hearing but, shy by nature, they usually disappear into the bush when they hear strange noises. They can distinguish colour, form, and movement, but their short-sightedness prevents them from seeing whether a person is approaching or retreating. Consequently, they regard every encounter as a threat. A bear may make a bluff charge to get a closer look and then stop and stand on its back legs to nose the air for a scent.

Current lore advises that during a charge you should stand your ground, otherwise the bear will just keep coming. But that's easier said than done when half a ton of angry animal is thundering towards you.

If the bear keeps coming, play dead and lie face down with hands over your head and neck, because bears usually maul the face. Trees north of 60 degrees latitude generally make good escape routes; spindly lodge pole pines and black spruce have small branches that bears find difficult to climb. Only a wide-bore rifle with a high-velocity bullet shot through the heart will kill a bear; anything less will just wound and enrage it. Flares, often carried for protection, are likely to set light to the bear's coat and madden it. Red pepper sprayed in a bear's eyes may deter it, but the bear has to be awfully close for it to be effective.

I know a man who was mauled in a river while fishing for salmon one fall. He held his breath and tried to stay under water, but each time he surfaced for air the bear took a swipe, eventually removing most of his scalp. His most vivid memory was of the bear's foul breath.

Geologists, who spend summers prospecting in the bush, sometimes end up in hospital after bear encounters. One man working with an exploration company near Atlin survived a vicious mauling by a bear. He was walking up a dry stream bed one morning when he surprised a grizzly. She knocked his pack off, grabbed his arm, and dragged him to the ground. She sniffed and pawed him, and then bit the side of his bowed head despite the fact that it was covered by his hands.

"I could hear teeth scraping across my skull," he told me in hospital. "After a couple of bites at my head, she started clawing my back. I screamed, but she rolled me over and stood over me."

He tried to kick the bear in the stomach but failed, so he grabbed a rock and beat her on the nose.

"She had foul breath. I don't think they brush their teeth," he said. "She'd been digging up roots nearby and had that earthy smell. She rolled me over once more, scraped some dirt over me, and left."

He lay on the ground until the bear had gone and then headed back to camp. Inspecting his wounds in a compass mirror, he saw that his face was bleeding profusely and a chunk of flesh was hanging from his thigh. A helicopter arrived, and his nightmare ended at the hospital.

He had multiple lacerations, the deepest around his shoulders, back, and buttocks; there was a full metre of lacerations on his scalp and face. His cheek bone was crushed. Within four days he was out of intensive care and, swathed in bandages, was sitting in a chair. One eye was sewn shut. I asked him if he regretted not carrying a rifle.

"During fifteen years working in the bush I've only seen six or seven bears at close range." he said. "I never carry a gun for fear of shooting myself accidentally, and when I'm laden with rock specimens, a rifle is too heavy to lug around."

One night, a black bear visited the camp of another geologist friend and ate twelve kilograms of dog food. The bear then climbed a nearby tree. As the geologist was chopping down the tree to chase him off, the frightened bear, full of dog food, released a deluge of faeces on his cap.

One fall, Sylvester Jack sent me an invitation to visit his fish camp on the Taku. I flew down with Clive Aspinall in his little yellow and red Luscombe float plane. Early morning cloud hung over Kuthai Lake and the upper reaches of Silver Salmon River. We swung around Mount O'Keefe and dropped into the Sloko Gorge, which debouches into the Nakina upstream from where the Inklin River joins it to become the Taku. This route, a traditional Indian trail, is now grown over.

We could see down the length of the Taku River, which cuts a gash through the Coastal Mountains — one of the few breaches in the mighty wall that cuts off the interior Yukon from the Pacific. The geography suddenly changes from the dry, arid Yukon plateau to lush green rainforest. The river, nudging up against steep cliffs, making oxbow channels, and spreading out into sloughs, weaves a braided course along the valley,

In the upper part of the valley, browns and golds predominate due to the many exposed sand bars and the rocky nature of the surrounding hills. Lower down towards the coast, green moose pastures appear, indicating a high yearly rainfall. Steep mountains fall to the edge of the Taku's laced stream, small glaciers hang from valleys high up in the mountains, and waterfalls pour over vertical cliffs. Farther down, some massive glaciers descend to the valley floor.

As we flew over the Inklin fish camp, a hillside above was still smoking from a recent fire that had scorched several hectares of forest. To our right, the Tulsequah River flowed out through a wide valley. Some huge wooden structures, the remains of the Polaris-Taku lead-zinc mine, stood opposite. Upstream, bright orange tailings of a more recent mine lay beside the mine adit. At the head of the valley, the snout of the Tulsequah Glacier flowed off the Juneau Icecap. Clive pointed out the homestead of a former Atlinite who had once built an elaborate vegetable garden and greenhouses over the warm springs near Atlin. With her husband and his four brothers, they now cultivate a large vegetable garden in this remote place.

Sylvester's fish camp stood eight kilometres downstream on Cranberry Island. As we circled to land on the river, we passed over a cut line that marked the international border with the United States. The muddy, glacial Taku River obscured dangerous floating logs and debris. As we taxied up to a dock at the lower end of the island, Sylvester appeared out of the bush and secured our line to a tree. He had close-cropped grizzled hair, a rounded face, and a burly frame like his brothers.

"Hi! Doc," he said. "Welcome to the Taku."

He led us along a path through the cottonwood forest to his house, perched on a high bank above the flooding river. Two aluminum river boats that Sylvester used for fishing were moored below. The house was surrounded by an assortment of junk: fishing tackle, floats, buoys, nets, gas cans, and old outboard motors. Beside the house, two plywood tent frames could accommodate overflow members of the family in summer.

The single room was thick with mosquitoes, even though several mosquito coils burned. Netting was hung over the beds. Sylvester's granddaughter, Charmaine, made coffee. Brought up by Sylvester and his wife, Evelyn, as their own daughter, she has been coming to the fish camp since she was eight. This pretty teenager appeared a most improbable fisherwoman.

We sat drinking strong coffee together with two relatives from a house at the other end of the island. They discussed fishing regulations and the over-fishing on the American side of the border that causes a paucity of fish to ever reach the upper reaches of the Taku.

"The salmon run's open at noon," said Sylvester. "We'd better go fetch some ice."

He took us to his boat, and, with the 55 horsepower jet engine set a full throttle, we roared off down the river. We crossed the United States border and raced on down towards Juneau, which lies a couple of hours away. The river was dotted with many forested islands, and small fishing outfits and weekend cabins stood among trees on the banks. Two wooden fish wheels were placed where the river narrows to catch the salmon for tagging by the fisheries officers.

Sylvester turned into a side channel up a fast-flowing creek and wove a course against the considerable current. Suddenly the enclosing banks parted, and we were in a basin with two gigantic glaciers flowing down into its head. There, the front face of the glacier calved, shedding massive icebergs. Sylvester approached the nearest iceberg and hacked off huge chunks of ice with an axe. Clive and I had great difficulty hauling the heavy ice on board and into the large cooler. When the box was full, we turned around and returned to the main Taku River.

"Long time ago, the river there flowed under an ice bridge to the sea," said Sylvester. "One of the chiefs entered the cavern to see what was on the other side. He disappeared. The onlookers cried out 'good courage,' but he was never seen again. You know, that ice in the cooler is 10,000 years old. It's crystalline, which makes it so clear."

We returned for more coffee at Sylvester's house. Charmaine had washed the dishes and had prepared sandwiches for lunch.

"I really miss my daughter," she said, a sad look clouding her beautiful face. "She's just two now. Grandma Evelyn looks after her in Atlin while I'm down here on the river fishing with Grandpa." Turning towards the stove she brushed tears from her eyes with the back of her hand.

She donned a brand-new pair of yellow waterproof pants and a stained, faded-yellow jacket. Jet-black hair hung straight from under a blue baseball cap, tipped back on her head. From the moment the fishing boat headed out into the strong current, the beautiful Charmaine became transformed from a gauche youth into a superbly competent fisherwoman.

She held the net in both hands and threw it, floats on one side and sinkers on the other, out over the bow. As Sylvester reversed the motor, she strung the net across half the river. Net and boat then drifted with the current. A flurry of tugging on the floats and splashing in the water indicated a catch. Charmaine started to haul in the net. She guessed that we had caught at least half a dozen fish; Sylvester wagered that we had more.

To extricate the slippery salmon, Charmaine wore white gloves, which, until they became blood-stained, gave her a ladylike appearance. She pulled a thrashing fish clear of the tangled net and killed it with a wooden club. It took Clive five attempts to kill one struggling fish, and Sylvester made some ribald remarks on the ineptitude of white men.

There were seven five-pounders in the first drift. By the time Sylvester turned the boat around and headed back upstream for

Sylvester Jack and Charmaine on the Taku River.

another drift, Charmaine, dexterous as any surgeon, had all the fish beheaded and gutted and ready for the ice box.

It turned out to be an excellent day in the nets. Other members of the family had landed one drift of seventeen fish. They boxed up the fish in ice and took them up to the landing where a plane from Atlin would fly them out to the fish buyers. Clive and I had to get back to Atlin. As we circled over the river to dip our wings in parting, we looked down on Sylvester and Charmaine, a remarkable grandfather/granddaughter team who had another six hours of fishing ahead of them.

In another camp I visited on the river later that year, some Tlingit Indians were smoking the season's fish — a family affair in which everyone took part. As with all extended Indian families, relatives of various ages hung around camp. Some worked gutting fish, others hauled the catch up from the river bank, and the younger ones played. A canvas wall tent, hung on a lodge pole pine frame, was set in a clump of willows a little way back from the bank. A tin stove-pipe, surrounded by a metal collar to protect the canvas from burning, protruded through the roof. Fish were hung to dry under a blue tarpaulin awning, strung over a wooden frame beside the tent. A small open fire made in a circle of stones burned constantly, providing smoke to keep the flies away.

A fish trap lay where the river made a large whirlpool at a turbulent eddy. A boom, made from several thin logs tied together, floated in the eddy line. One end was held to the bank by a rope. It angled out, hanging between the opposing currents. To this boom was attached a net with its bottom side weighted.

The king (or chinook) salmon run for about eight weeks on their way back to the creeks where they hatched four to seven years before. How they find their way up from the ocean to their birthplace is a mystery. Smell may be the secret; if the olfactory nerve, which provides the fish's sense of smell, is cut, the salmon never returns. Tasty sockeye salmon come after the kings; coho stay until later in the large ocean estuaries like that of the Taku.

On their journey upstream from the ocean, the salmon rest in eddies before heading out to battle fast flowing currents. They meet their doom in these eddies if a fish camp is nearby. The prize catch that morning was a thirty kilogram king salmon, longer from nose to tail than the ten-year-old boy who drew the boom by a rope to empty the net on the bank. Its scales had a silvery-black sheen and its pink gills still gasped for air. Some of the other fish were mottled from battles fought with strong currents on the way upstream.

The boy dumped the fish in a pile in the shade of a willow bush at the top of the bank. One of the female elders hauled out a big salmon and tossed it onto a bed of leafy, green twigs. Bright orange-red clusters of eggs and pale fawn roes of the female salmon hung on a pole frame. Squatting, the elder drew a piece of tarpaulin over her knees to keep her dress clean. She wielded her sharp knife deftly,

forearm muscles taut and movements honed by years of practice —
a skill none of the younger women could match.

"Don't you ever cut yourself?" I asked.

"Not much," she replied. "My meat good. Heal quick."

Out came the guts and the roes. Then she split open the dorsal
vein and removed the blood. She thrust the knife into the gills and
parted the head from the body.

"Best part of fish," she said. "Boil him and suck on his bones.
No good for white man."

The evisceration complete, she carried the huge fish over to the
smoke tent and slapped it on a rickety table, pink fleshy side up.
With another even sharper knife she cut the meat in long strips,
down to the skin. She hung the flayed fish on washing lines suspended across the fire to dry for three or four days. The colour of
the drying fish under the tarpaulin was a rich salmon pink.

"Bear sometimes he smell fish across the river," she said. "He
come swimming across to eat. That's why we keep loaded gun in
tent."

I could understand why fish camp features so prominently in
the childhood memories of most Indian adults; I would have been
happy to spend time there myself.

Fall began to turn to winter. By late October ice fog had
shrouded the town for a month, formed when the lake churned and
turned over, bringing the cold water to the surface. Low air temperatures caused steam from the lake to cement new snowflakes to
every tree branch; hoar-frost and freezing fog rimed the aspens and
willows, which stood leafless and naked. Then ice suddenly gripped
the lake and transformed it into a white sheet. The fog disappeared.
Spruce trees put on a winter coat, their branches curtseying under
the weight of fresh snow. The sun set on the mountain across the
wide Taku River delta, where several thousand bald eagles perched
to catch the fall salmon run. Snow lay on sand bars, but the river
water still flowed down to the sea. Weary old salmon swam up-

stream, shuddering and gasping. Their journey had been easier than that of the Yukon salmon, some of which have to ascend 3,000 kilometres of the Yukon River to die in spawning creeks on the M'Clintock River.

Some bald eagles, standing on the snow beside the river, were tucked up for the night, their wings wrapped like cloaks around their shoulders. Others perched in the branches of cottonwood trees across the river. Wise old eagles, white heads looking like snow, stood on driftwood logs on sand bars. Each bird had its territory. Mature white-cowled birds waved their huge wings to scare off cheeky brown-coated youngsters. Some birds balanced on the bodies of dead fish, pinned them with their talons, and tore at the flesh with curved, yellow beaks.

The snow on the bank beside the pecked carcasses was blood-stained and littered with guts. Dorsal fins of salmon carved the water surface that rippled as fish shuddered in their death throes. Birds on the bank waited patiently for the fish to die. As the birds flew off to savour a morsel, undisturbed by prying neighbours, their wide wings flapped lazily, with terminal feathers spread like fingers.

Bald eagles thrive along the coasts of south-east Alaska and British Columbia, where the world's largest concentrations of the birds live during the fall salmon-spawning season. Eagles prefer to roost in old-growth cottonwood trees beside rivers where they can forage abundant food, but in severe storms they move into the Sitka spruce and hemlock of the coniferous forests to shelter from the wind. They hang around gravel bars, sinister as vultures, to scavenge carrion. But there they are prey to older, bigger pirate birds that swoop down on their smaller, weaker fellows and steal their food.

In winter, when food is scarce, bald eagles either fly south to balmier climes, or they conserve their energy by perching asleep and only foraging off in flight for a few minutes of each day. Thus, idleness is the key to an eagle's winter survival. The ephemeral supply of their food and damage to the rivers by clear-cut logging and toxic mine tailings are their greatest threats.

A host of other birds shared the river with the eagles in a well-established hierarchy: ravens got second pickings, seagulls the leftovers. Ducks and other waterfowl were set apart from the drama being enacted around them and went about their business unheeding.

Heavy mist settled in the valley, insinuating itself along the delta. Distant, newly snow-clad mountains glowed in the fading rays of the sun. The eagles are a northern marvel, like the migration of the Porcupine caribou herd, the spring arrival of swans, and the king salmon run.

✦✦✦

Body & Soul

Fall is one of our favourite seasons for the drive down to Atlin. The leaves on deciduous trees change to yellow, snow dusts the hilltops, and the mosquitoes and black flies have gone. A tang in the air tells us that skiing cannot be far off.

On arriving in town, I raise a flag on a high flagpole beside the cabin to let people know I am available for medical emergencies. At first, I used the "P" flag , a white square on a blue background meaning, in the International Code of Signals, "All aboard. Vessel about to depart." Though often true, this seemed inappropriate, so I replaced it with the diagonal white on blue St. Andrew's Cross, which denotes the letter "M." This letter indicates that there is a "Doctor Aboard."

Atlin has a small Red Cross outpost hospital staffed by two nurses who manage the bulk of the town's daily medical problems. A doctor from one of the Whitehorse medical clinics pays a monthly visit to see patients at the outpost. Any patients who cannot be treated in Atlin are sent to Whitehorse in an ambulance that is driven by volunteers — mostly members of the fire department. Since Whitehorse takes three hours to reach by ambulance, in an emergency the nurses can charter a plane or a helicopter.

Nursing in a remote community is an exacting and nerve-wracking job. Nurses may have to treat a severely ill or injured person and must try to keep them alive until they can reach a hospital. Although conditions have improved since the early days, nurses still bear a heavy responsibility; they work alone and far from help.

Medical care in Atlin started when the Reverend John Pringle pitched a small hospital tent beside his own tent. That winter, he could do little more than prescribe raw onions and raw potatoes to "poor men broken down under the frightful hardships and suffering from scurvy." The next year, he wrote to the Klondyke Nurses' Committee of the Presbyterian Church of Canada in Toronto and asked for two nurses to care for sick and dying miners.

Describing a building that he found to serve as a home for the sick he wrote, "Lying in a low cot was the man I had come to see, and on pole bunks around were five others, injured and diseased. At the door was a rough box with a dead body in it, and outside was another."

Two Ontario ladies, Elizabeth Mitchell and Helen Bone, answered the trumpet call and left for Atlin. The Government Agent gave them a cabin with a mud roof to serve as a hospital. One very cold night, the Reverend Pringle visited the hospital and found one of the nurses wearing her fur coat and tending three patients who lay on canvas cots crowded around a sheet-iron stove in the middle of the sawdust-covered floor. This spectacle inspired him to collect funds to build a proper hospital.

Volunteer townspeople built St. Andrew's Hospital under the direction of an Aberdonian Scottish carpenter. Soon afterwards, they erected a nurses' residence, which still stands opposite the Courthouse and is owned by John Harvey, the McKee Creek miner. For three years, nurses Mitchell and Bone treated an unending stream of patients, many with bizarre conditions rarely seen in Toronto. Eventually they resigned, worn out by hard work under exacting conditions. A succession of nurses and doctors came and went over succeeding years until 1954, when the Red Cross took over the present Glaciological Institute and turned it into a hospital.

Major Neville with his dogs and water cart, and nurses Mitchell and Bone, outside Saint Andrews Church and the hospital. *(Yukon Archives/Atlin Historical Society Collection, No. 84/50-A73)*

In the early days, guardians of body and spirit worked hand in hand. For six years, the Reverend Fred Stephenson provided medical and spiritual care to the people of Atlin. Typical of a breed of young muscular evangelicals from Oxford and Cambridge Universities, he had studied medicine in England, but had dropped out after two years because of eye trouble. He emigrated to British Columbia, studied for the church, became ordained, and enrolled in the Diocese of Caledonia, which posted him to northern British Columbia. When the gold rush started, he moved to Atlin, where the country and the people were similar to his previous parish.

Stephenson held services in tents or buildings of various merchants and hoteliers in town. On Sunday evening, he would walk fifteen kilometres to Discovery to minister to the Pine Creek miners in a large marquee, which was used during the week as a saloon and

gambling hall. Before the service, he would have to collect playing cards that had been thrown on the sawdust floor during the
previous night's poker game. Once he worshipped in a store, where
the congregation sat on a row of makeshift lumber benches. As the
hymn before the sermon was thumped out on an English
concertina organ, the front bench collapsed, and row upon row of
burly miners fell backwards like dominoes and landed in a heap on
the floor.

With his wife and child, Stephenson first lived in a tent and then
moved to a single storey frame building with walls of rough lumber and canvas on the floor. To supplement his meagre stipend, he
worked as a carpenter three days a week and hauled water on his
own from the lake rather than buy it from the Atlin Canine Waterworks.

An early diarist described him to be "of middle height, clean
shaven, spare, and hard as nails. He could race a fast dog team or
keep up with the best of trail walkers. He was a good shot and could
live off the country if need be. Round camp, he would do any
chores, were they bucking or splitting wood, cooking, or washing
up. He was a good storyteller round the fire when the pipes were
lit. He gave first aid when required and was one who ministered
rather than preached."

When acting as magistrate in northern British Columbia.,
Stephenson arraigned a young Indian Lothario who had seduced
several maidens of his tribe. Stephenson found the young man guilty
in court in the face of damning evidence and sentenced him to "im-
mediate surgery." Stephenson's medical school experience enabled
him to fake sterilizing some instruments. He ordered the man to
lie down on the "operating table" and with a dramatic gesture held
a scalpel over the offending organ. The young man repented and
swore never to misbehave again, whereupon he was set free.

At the turn of the century, Stephenson organized a collection
for money to build a proper church. The churchwarden, a bank
manager, always took the collection at evensong. He was usually

absent from morning service, either because he had slept in or because he had taken the minister's dog to hunt partridges. One day, he solicited a fellow bank manager.

"D'you want to get in on a real live proposition?" asked the churchwarden.

"Can you recommend it?" replied his colleague.

"I should say so. It's the surest thing this side of the grave."

"Are you in on it?"

"Up to the eyes and then some."

"How much is it going to cost?"

"Fifty a share and sure interest on your money."

"OK, I'll flutter a couple of fifties."

The churchwarden then handed the other bank manager a list of subscribers with the bank manager's name already inscribed at the top.

The people of Atlin collected $1,025, and St. Martin's Anglican Church was constructed entirely with timber from a local mill. Built on the corner of Trainor and Third, St. Martin's was one of the few buildings to survive the devastating fires of 1914 and 1916. In 1901, Bishop Bompas, the first bishop of the diocese of Selkirk (later the Yukon), held the inaugural service on Trinity Sunday.

One Sunday, Stephenson was christening the first-born son of the Atlin Tlingit Chief Taku Jack, who stood at the font with his wife and baby. Stephenson asked what name they had chosen.

"We call 'im Jesus Christ," said Taku Jack.

"That would be sacrilege," said the priest. "You must choose another name."

"We call 'im J. H. Brownlee then," replied the chief. Brownlee was a local mining engineer and notorious gambler.

In 1906, Stephenson was transferred from Atlin. He mushed three dogs 1,500 kilometres south to his next parish, near Smithers in the Bulkley Valley.

An interregnum lasted for nineteen years, with ordained priests visiting occasionally. Ex-sea captain Hathorne and ex-army major

Neville held the congregation together during the severe Spanish influenza epidemic that reached Atlin in March 1920. Thirteen people died. Mothers tried boiling balsam bark to give to their children to drink instead of water, but to no avail. The scourge, which killed more people worldwide than did the entire First World War, wiped out a third of the native population of Atlin a year later.

The Catholic Church had its highs and its lows in Atlin. The most recent incumbent, Father Joseph Plaine, became a regular visitor to our cabin at tea time. With no one to repair his clothes, his sleeve cuffs and trouser turn-ups of fading black cloth were frayed and scuffed, his dog collar was off-white, and his grey pullover was threadbare at the elbows. In winter, he abandoned clerical garb for a pair of worsted wool pants, known locally as "Jimmy Gees" (after an old-timer who wore pants of that style year-round). Outdoors, Father wore an old leather flying cap with ear flaps fastened under his chin. Over everything was a padded army coat, the hood framed by a scrawny piece of rabbit fur.

One evening, Father Plaine and I spent two hours together in front of the picture window watching a fall sunset paint vermilion patterns across the sky, the mood and hue changing by the minute.

In French, he told me stories of his younger days. He was born at Rennes, which is tucked into the armpit of Brittany. He entered the Oblate priesthood and emigrated to Canada. At the outbreak of World War II, gendarmes, ordered to gather young men to serve in the French army, visited his home and confronted his mother.

"Where's your son, Joseph?" they asked.

"You can't get him," she replied. "He's in Canada."

The gendarmerie contacted the RCMP who demanded that Joseph see a doctor to certify whether or not he was fit for military service. He failed the medical exam.

Father Plaine spent two years in Telegraph Creek on the Stikine River in northern British Columbia. There, an old Indian taught him to use snowshoes, but the young priest found them awkward and took them off. Floundering in the snow, he was upbraided by the Indian: "Keep you snowshoes on or you'll never make it through this snow." He followed that advice, and he went on to become a skilled northern traveller.

He was sent to Mayo, where one winter the thermometer plummeted to minus 58 degrees Celsius. The local silver mines at Keno and Elsa were closed because of the war, and times were hard. For five years, he took the place of Father Alec Esperance, a tough man who came into the country with the gold rush.

"Esperance once was sick with a high fever in the hospital in Mayo," said Father Plaine. "The doctor told him he was dying. When the doctor went to the kitchen for coffee, Esperance hopped out of bed and pretended to go to the lavatory. He disappeared through the window into the minus 40 degree night. By next day his fever was gone and he felt fine again."

Father Plaine's next ministry was in the Mackenzie River Delta. He learned the language of the Gwich'in Indian communities of Fort McPherson and Arctic Red River. Then, with guides, he travelled by dog sled from Fort McPherson to Old Crow, where he was to take charge of the first Catholic mission. They crossed the divide of the Richardson Mountains by way of Rat Pass and Summit Lake, joined the headwaters of the Bell, a tributary of the Porcupine River, and travelled downstream to Old Crow.

Despite his small frame and frail appearance, he travelled widely in the wilderness. Soon after arriving in Old Crow, he set out on a winter journey to visit Herschel Island, on the Yukon's north coast, to say mass for the men at the Distant Early Warning Line (DEWline) radio base. He was accompanied by RCMP Inspector Fraser, who was on patrol with three guides: two Indian and one Inuit. They had arranged to meet the Herschel Island Mountie at the halfway point. Leaving the Old Crow Flats, they came to a canyon where the Firth River cut through to the Beaufort Sea. The Indian guides spotted overflow water lying on top of the ice.

"Don't go down there, Father," they said. "It's dangerous."

The Indians were comfortable with snowshoes in the woods, but not on ice. The Inuit, wearing sealskin boots, was quite at home on ice. Father Plaine was not deterred and, following the Inspector, his dog sled shot over the edge and down the steep bank towards the river. Father hung on, jammed his foot on the brake to try to slow the careening sled, and reached the bottom in one piece.

They met the Mountie from Herschel at a trapper's cabin at the edge of the timberline on the Alaskan border. The trapper, facing starvation after a very poor season, had gone to Aklavik for food. All they found in the cabin were some sticks of prospector's dynamite and a single spring bed without a mattress. The Inuit guide promptly lay down on it.

Inspector Fraser chided him. "It's a shame Father has to sleep on the floor while you've taken the only bed." So the Inuit vacated the spot and rolled himself in his sleeping blanket underneath the bed on which the Father and the Inspector lay. At 2 a.m. they were awoken by the loud snoring of the Eskimo and were unable to get back to sleep.

When Father Plaine was travelling back from Herschel Island, accompanied only by the Inuit guide, he ran into a raging blizzard.

"God, help me now," he prayed. " I'm seventeen miles from my goal and I need you."

Unable to see more than a few yards ahead, they set off into the storm. They were aiming for the Firth River, which would lead them back in the right direction for Old Crow.

"When I stop, you stop," the Inuit guide told him. "In two hours we'll be at the river." After two hours steady walk, the guide pointed into the murky gloom. "See that black spot over there?" he asked. "That's the way to go." A few minutes later, they stood on the banks of the Firth River exactly where a break in the escarpment led down to the ice.

Father Plaine spent three years in Old Crow. Then he returned to France for the first time in seventeen years. He found the language very confusing; there were many new slang words. His family had difficulty understanding him, and his sister complained of his terrible accent. He returned to Dawson City for three years and then, in 1961, went to Atlin, where he ministered for 30 years.

Most weekends when we were down at the cabin, I would call in at the Catholic rectory for a chat and another story. Father Plaine's stories, so modestly told, always confirmed my admiration for this remarkable man who had devoted so much of his life to the people of the north — often with few tangible results.

Pilots

While the church was important to the spiritual life of early Atlin settlers, airplanes soon became their lifeline to the outside. Before 1950, when the road linked the town to the Alaska Highway, the alternative to air travel was the long and expensive rail and lake route to Atlin.

George Simmons, a pioneering aviator, opened Northern Airways in Carcross and operated a regular service from Dawson City to Vancouver. Atlin was among the many stops. Northern Airways also won the Royal Mail contract between Carcross and Atlin. This rang the death-knell of the overland dog sled and horse sleigh service for which George Simmons, at age 12, had been an assistant mail driver.

Herman Peterson, now an octogenarian and a living legend, appeared on the Atlin scene in 1949. Of medium height and stocky build, he still has a full head of crinkled, wiry gray hair. Green work pants and a green shirt are still his daily uniform. His weather-beaten fingers are finely tuned to work at lathe and workbench, where he is a master craftsman. All summer long, Herman, a certified mechanic and engineer, tinkers with his two small planes to keep them in top condition, although nowadays he flies infrequently and purely for pleasure.

In winter, he makes violins. Inspired by a champion Yukon fiddler, Herman taught himself to play the fiddle. Then he decided to build his own violin. But first he had to make the precision tools for turning and scalloping the front and back sound boards from a single block of wood. His first instrument, a Guaneri copy, took two years to make. At last count, this latter-day Stradivarius had made seventeen violins.

On first meeting, Herman is reserved and diffident, but soon his sombre face melts in a friendly smile. Unstintingly generous with his time and expertise, he is never happier than when confronted by a friend with a mechanical problem. And I have often been that person. He leads me out to his workshop, which is located in a clapboard shed in a corner of his garden. Inside are lathes, metal presses, grinding and planing machines, and an array of bottles and boxes holding all manner and size of nuts, bolts, and screws. Parts of old airplanes are scattered around the shop just in case, one day, they may come in useful. Once the problem is diagnosed, he sets about building the part needed to fix it on the lathe in his shop. He has redesigned the rudder for my boat and has made several modifications to it.

Herman was born in Denmark and emigrated to Canada as a boy. Even before he had a pilot's licence, he bought a Simon Spartan CF-ABC. Depression was at its peak and, with money being scarce, he and a friend barnstormed in country districts, charging $1.50 a flight. While working for his commercial licence, he apprenticed as a welder in Toronto and nearly ended his flying career when carbide exploded in his eyes. He bears the scars to this day, but by sheer luck they only affect the upper half of his vision.

When Northern Airways advertised for bush pilots, Herman applied against the advice of a pilot friend who said, "Don't go up there. The runway's so short you have to jump off the end to get up flying speed." Nevertheless, he and his wife, Doris, moved to Carcross where he flew the mail for George Simmons in a Waco ZQC-6. "Ma" Simmons, a loving person who reputedly could "talk

The mail plane in front of the White Pass Hotel. *(Barr Airphoto, Juneau)*

to a tramp yet fit in with the Queen," adopted the young Petersons as her own family.

The construction of the Alaska Highway provided lots of work for local aviation businesses. It was a busy time for Northern Airways, which chartered three extra aircraft. Herman flew road engineers up and down the highway and piloted American top brass on inspection tours. He also searched the bush for several crash-landed planes.

Herman loves telling the stories of his early adventures, and I often go down to his house and just sit and listen, gently encouraging them to flow.

"In 1949, I decided to go out on my own," he said. "So I applied for a license to operate a commercial flying business from Atlin. While waiting for my licence to be processed, I worked as handyman on the *S. S. Tutshi*. Doris and I founded Peterson's Air Service, but we soon changed the name to Coast Range Airways."

Herman flew prospectors and miners all over the region in various planes: an Aeronca Sedan, a Cessna 170 and 180, a Fairchild 71, a De Haviland Beaver, and an Otter. For 25 years, in all conditions, he flew the mail weekly to Telegraph Creek and to Tulsequah twice a week. The Coastal Range is unpredictable because oceanic disturbances roll in from the Gulf of Alaska and creeping cloud hangs in valleys like the Taku. Juneau, where much of the mail originated, was often socked in with rain and fog. Herman, however, not only never missed a run, but he was late only once — and that was because of bad weather.

Herman, who knows intimately the history of flying out of Atlin — he himself being very much part of that history — never tires of telling stories about the early planes and their pilots.

The *Queen of the Yukon* was the first airplane to land in Atlin (in April 1928). She was sister ship to the *Spirit of St. Louis*, which Charles Lindbergh used to crossed the Atlantic. The following year, Atlin citizens collected money and, using a local grader and their own hands, built an 1,800 foot runway on the old road to Discovery City.

A tragic event occurred near Teslin (northeast of Atlin). "Paddy" Burke, a pioneer northern bush pilot, piloted the first passenger flight from the Lower 48 to Alaska. He had received his "wings" in the Royal Flying Corps during the Arab Revolt and had flown all over the Middle East after World War I. In August 1930, flying a Junkers F13, he made a forced landing on the ice at Wolf Lake. The plane quickly froze in so, with his mechanic, Emil Kading, and "Three Fingers" Bob Martin, a prospector passenger, he started to walk out towards Teslin. It would take another sixty terrible days and nights until they were spotted by a search plane. Kading and Martin were barely alive, and Burke had died earlier of starvation and exposure. The same year, another Junkers ran off the short Atlin strip. The incident convinced residents to further widen, lengthen, and clear the approaches to the field.

Herman Peterson as a young man.

In the 1930s, J.H. Eastman II flew across the continent on a gold-seeking expedition to the Liard Valley. He didn't find much gold, but he caught a bad case of gold fever. He founded the Detroit Aircraft Corporation, designed the E-2 Sea Rover flying boat, and built thirty of them before the company went bankrupt and was taken over by Lockheed. The next year, he acquired the last five of the E-2 flying boats and, with a crew of airmen adventurers, flew to Tulsequah, which became his base for trips into the Liard country. Eastman moved the operation to Atlin, where he took options on mining claims on Spruce Creek. Along with some wealthy backers, he formed the Columbia Development Mining Corporation and went into mining seriously.

During his long flying career, Herman had many adventures, but he had few serious incidents.

"Once, returning from Frances Lake in an old Fairchild on floats," he told me, "the lower hinge on my rudder broke loose flying at 1,000 feet. "The rudder jumped off its post and fixed the plane in a hard left turn over a beaver swamp. I just missed the treetops at ninety miles per hour. One wing hit the water, the plane spun round, and I grazed the top of my head on the compass bracket."

He was well warmed up now and I could not, nor did I want to, stop him.

"It was in the fall of 1953 — September, I think," he said. "I was flying my Aeronca Sedan over a 4,500-foot pass near Kiniskan Lake on the way to Stewart, British Columbia. The plane suddenly lost height in turbulent air. I couldn't turn round, so I put down on a creek bed of coarse gravel. I walked away from that one."

For six days he walked towards Telegraph Creek. His 30-kilogram pack included emergency gear, log books, food, and a tarpaulin. It rained every day, and he was constantly wet from struggling through dripping buck brush. Once, he heard a plane flying over, so he emptied a can of aviation fuel under a couple of dead spruce trees and set fire to them. His beacon went unnoticed. He walked in cut-down rubber boots, which were adequate on level ground, but useless on steep hills. He had severe blisters when he emerged at Telegraph Creek, but was otherwise in good shape.

"Let's go down and look at the dock," said Herman, always keen to show off his current project. "The rails aren't running smoothly. I think they need some work."

Herman's two-seater Luscombe is secured to an ingenious movable dock, which he designed and built in front of his house. The plane's floats rest on a small platform, which he can raise or lower by a crank-operated ratchet. To adjust the platform to the lake level, a cable hauls the dock, which runs on small wheels, up and down rails set on the shore. The plane has a 150-horsepower engine and extra buoyant floats. Painted orange-yellow with a red stripe down the fuselage and a chequered tail plane, it carries the original colours of Peterson's Air Service.

Herman has spent the greater part of his lifetime in the air; now, he finds his fun in tinkering. His biplane *Susie,* which took 2,000 hours to build in the shed beside his house, has a gross weight of 1,000 pounds and cruises at 120 miles per hour. He is so busy keeping his planes in pristine condition that he rarely has time to fly. On most Canada Days, however, he complements the ground parade by flying a few loops, rolls, and spins over the town.

Occasionally I can lure him away from endless maintenance jobs to fly over the lake shore so that I can take photographs to supplement my home-made navigational chart. I have to shoehorn myself into the right-hand seat — my knees against the instrument panel. Utterly at home in his own medium, Herman controls the joystick with finger and thumb like a conductor's baton. The naming of the realigned Atlin airport to Peterson's Field is a fitting accolade to this distinguished flyer.

Herman owned one of the first sailboats on the lake: the *Arctic Tern*. This 25-foot Ericson sloop has a drop-keel centreboard that can be raised when mooring on a shelving beach. A superb pilot, Herman expected sailing would be much the same as flying, but without an instructor he never became truly confident, especially in reefing the sails. He and Doris frightened themselves a few times out in the boat in strong winds with too much sail up, and they never got the pleasure they hoped for. He eventually sold *Arctic Tern* to fellow pilot Arden Hixson. Being a man of toys, Herman ordered a tippy 14-foot dinghy, which is even less suitable for someone a little stiff in the joints. He sailed her solo round Fourth Island rock in a whitecap wind as if to prove he could do it. Now, when he sails with me, he enjoys the freedom of not being skipper.

Herman has become a close friend, and we are never happier than when we mess around together in his workshop — often building some small part for my sailboat. Occasionally, we go flying. Doris benignly watches as the boys indulge their passion for toys.

Another legendary Atlin bush pilot was Dick Bond, a fly-by-the-seat-of-the-pants cowboy of the air — poles apart from

Herman Peterson. Dick always wore a faded blue baseball cap over curly ginger hair, brushed back from a deeply furrowed forehead. The skin of his face was greasy and pock-marked.

He drove around town hunched over the wheel of a battered red truck, his left arm resting on the rolled-down window. He would stop to chat with friends in between long drags of the cigarette that was always alight between his nicotine-brown fingers. Long years of smoking had ravaged his breathing with chronic bronchitis and emphysema, so he would break into paroxysms of coughing that brought conversation to a halt. Then he would straighten himself up, grin, and say: "I must give these damned things up. I've cut down from three packs to two this week." His attempts to quit smoking never lasted long, and the only time I remember him without a cigarette is when he was loading fuel into his plane.

Dick came to Atlin after flying for several years in the bush of northern British Columbia under conditions that would make pilots from the balmy south cringe. His licence was valid only for aerial spraying around Whitehorse, so he applied for a licence to carry passengers and goods out of Atlin. But since there were two carriers in the region, he was turned down. Despite being served a "cease and desist order" he kept on flying commercially. He would fly anyone, any place, any time in the long days and never-dark nights of summer. He cheekily advertised his company in the local paper as "Your Friendly Chisel Airways."

Dick's company, Taku Air, owned a beat-up old Beaver on floats, the type of workhorse that helped open up Canada's wilderness north of 60 degrees latitude. I was familiar with the solid and forgiving features of the Beaver from working in Labrador many years before with the flying doctor service of the Grenfell Association. Dick came to life in the left-hand captain's seat and displayed skills acquired in a lifetime of flying small planes on wheels, floats, or skis. He would land on short, bumpy dirt strips, on small lakes, and on

Dick Bond.

glaciers. In the rugged country where he flew, map reading is difficult because of featureless terrain and often atrocious weather.

To carry freight, Dick took out all the seats and loaded the plane with drums, crates, and luggage until the floats sat low in the water. Like many bush pilots, he flew overloaded to make his money for the year in the short summer season. From the deck of the cabin, we often watched his run up when the plane was so heavy it couldn't get up onto the float-step until well out past First Island. Once off the water, the engine laboured as the plane slowly gained height. When commercial fishing began to thrive on the Taku River, Dick flew salmon out to Atlin, where it was iced or smoked. Rumour had it that even the plane's floats were filled with fish.

Because of his bad safety record, Dick waged an ongoing battle with government inspectors from the Department of Transport. He habitually infringed or ignored regulations. Once, he lost his undercarriage taking off from a sandbar on the Taku River, but he never reported the incident. Inspectors often paid unannounced and unwelcome visits to check his weight-and-balance records and his air maintenance log, and several times they closed down his operation.

In 1978, Dick was flying in the mountains with an Atlin boy who was not buckled in and was sitting on a spare propeller. Dick crashed trying to turn around in cloud at the head of a blind valley. The boy died and Dick was severely injured. He was charged on six counts: flying recklessly, flying contrary to Visual Flight Rules, failing to provide seat belts, failing to secure cargo, not carrying adequate emergency equipment, and not carrying additional winter survival gear for flying over sparsely populated areas. He was fined $1,450 and his license was suspended for two years. He was later charged with a total of 210 counts of breaking Department of Transport regulations. Dick plead guilty to two charges and was fined $2,000.

Dick flew long hours; he took only short breaks while the plane was being loaded and refuelled. He would grab a strong cup of coffee in the hut that was the company's operations base on the dock and then would head off into the air again. When summer forest fires broke out, he would fly night and day to deliver canisters of fire retardant and the freight needed to maintain a camp for the fire crew.

Shortly after I got my pilot's licence, I went with Dick to Muddy Lake to help unload several barrels of fuel for a mining operation. I was itching to get my hands on the controls of the Beaver. As soon as we took off, Dick pointed out our course on the map, swung the control arm across to my side, and promptly fell asleep, snoring and gasping for air in his corner. His emphysema was getting worse and he would cough himself into fits of apoplexy that left him exhausted. When the Shesley airstrip came into view, I reluctantly dug him in the ribs to mobilize him for landing.

A government proposal to realign the old airport runway caused a controversy in town in which Dick was fully embroiled. The old runway ran parallel to the Surprise Lake Road a couple of miles outside town, just beyond the Pioneer Cemetery. The axis ran roughly east-west across the prevailing southerly wind. The landing path skimmed the treetops directly over an easterly bluff of Pine Creek Canyon. Dick was quite happy with the runway as it stood and resented the expense of rebuilding and lengthening it to 4,000 feet. As is common with debates in small towns, people became polarized and the issue contentious. Despite Dick's admonitions, a newly aligned runway was eventually built.

Dick later befriended Teresa Hunt, who owned the Food Basket grocery store directly across from our cabin. A petite, dynamic woman, she earned her commercial licence and flew many hours for Taku Air. They married and had a devoted, if stormy, relationship. Dick's health worsened steadily, and he gave up flying when his breathing became so shallow he could no longer load or unload freight. Teresa took over most of the flying operations of Taku Air in the Beaver and the Cessna 206 and nursed Dick through his protracted and miserable ill health.

During Dick's final illness, I visited him at least once a month in his trailer home a block away from the dock where his plane was tied. He would sit with a mug of strong black coffee in his hand and an ashtray full of butts beside him. He became so breathless, he would grasp the table with both hands to hold his chest rigid. Prolonged and violent coughing spasms turned him blue around the lips, and he became pale as a bed sheet from lack of oxygen. But he was always cheerful.

"Sorry, Pete," he would say apologetically, as he lit up another cigarette. "I'll give up this time and then it'll be better." He knew it was a lie, but we kept up the pretence because that was the way he wanted it.

On September 27, 1986, Teresa was chartered to fly to Dease Lake. The passengers were Al Passarel, the Member of the B.C. Legislative Assembly for the Stikine region (which includes Atlin) and his wife, Ruth. Also on board were Joe Florence, Ben Abel, and Shelley Smith.

Dease Lake was glassy calm. The child of a local pilot, accustomed to watching for her father's plane, was looking out of the window and noticed that the Atlin plane made an unusually steep approach and failed to level and flare for a normal landing. The plane plunged into the lake and sunk immediately in deep water. All on board drowned except Teresa. Although unable to swim, she floated to the surface through the shattered front windscreen and was rescued by a boat from the float plane dock. Apart from a few scratches, she was unhurt.

A coroner's inquest concluded that the accident was caused by a faulty landing. When landing on glassy water, experienced pilots judge the height of the plane above the surface by over flying, stirring ripples close along the shore, and watching for birds or flotsam as reference points. Teresa was far out on the lake.

The tragedy devastated Atlin. Despite Teresa's personal anguish, the investigations, the threat of lawsuits, and the opprobrium of the town, she tried to carry on with a normal life. She ran her store, drove the ambulance, and looked after Dick, whose emphysema steadily worsened, but whose loyalty to her never faltered.

Dick's life ebbed away in paroxysms of coughing that left him gasping and speechless. I witnessed his metamorphosis from a cocky, daredevil, chain-smoking, bush pilot to a cantankerous shadow. Hunched over the table and hooked by nose-prongs to an oxygen cylinder, he struggled for every breath, day and night, for months on end. He had tried many times to quit smoking, but each attempt ended with him feeling worse than before. Finally, the courage he showed in other sectors of his life disappeared, and despair overcame him. He died and was buried in Atlin's new Pioneer Cemetery. His grave site, high on an esker, overlooks both the airport and the town he knew so well.

Dick had planned his funeral to be a quiet affair. Nevertheless, the tiny Roman Catholic church that stands on the point of the harbour was packed to bursting. Forty people waited outside in minus 20 degrees Celsius sunshine; the community had silently absolved Dick, who was so often the focus of polemic. Father Plaine stoked wood into the oil-drum stove and then donned his surplice to conduct the service. The pall-bearers carefully negotiated the icy front steps of the church and then squeezed through the narrow, hingeless gate to reach the hearse. Father Plaine's only concession to the cold was a battered fur hat that he had worn on long dog sled journeys many years ago.

The cortege wound slowly past the fire hall, the Courthouse — scene of Dick's many battles with the law — and on past the Old Pioneer Cemetery, where several early pilots are buried with propellers atop their graves.

From the grave side, we looked out across the new airport, which Dick had never wanted, to Atlin Mountain towering over the lake. Shafts of sunlight penetrated fog that rose from a patch of open water in Torres Channel. Many townsfolk were at the grave side. Father Plaine said the requiem, the Anglican minister read the Twenty-third Psalm, Teresa placed Dick's blue flying cap on the coffin, and he was lowered into the ground.

Then everyone adjourned to the Atlin Inn for a party that Dick, who had been sober for twenty-one years, had already paid for "in order that my friends will enjoy themselves." Across the harbour a team of twelve dogs headed home — a lone musher swinging his kicking leg as his sled sped across the ice. At dusk, Sarah and I drove back to Whitehorse. The prices on the gas station billboard were replaced by large letters that read, "Good-bye Dick Bond, great bush pilot and Northerner".

Teresa began to get back on her feet again and was partially accepted back into a community that was divided over the blame for her accident. She took a paramedic course in Vancouver and began studying for exams to enter nursing school. Then she sold the store to give her some money to pay her legal fees. Within a month of Dick's death, Teresa's father died and she returned to England to bury him.

One winter's day shortly after her return, Teresa flew as a passenger in a Cessna 207 for an ambulance meeting in Dease Lake. The weather in Atlin was only fair. The pilot, recently arrived from the Prairies, took off and headed out on the route that Teresa herself had flown many times. The plane flew into cloud and crashed against Llangorse Mountain, 30 kilometres from Atlin. Everyone on board was killed.

The era of the northern bush pilot is rapidly passing. Mining has traditionally been their biggest employer, but the ways mines are serviced are changing. Nowadays, miners bulldoze roads across the wilderness and build airstrips to take bigger planes; the DC3s or the gigantic Hercules can carry as heavy a load as any bush plane at less cost. So we must say farewell to that generation of fearless flyers who were able to land small planes on tight strips and lakes deep in the bush.

Mail Run

The dog sled drivers who kept mail flowing through this wilderness between 1902 and 1933, often in hazardous circumstances and in all weathers, have became part of Atlin's folklore. Mail was tremendously important to Atlinites in those days when the town was cut off from the outside world. The first message had passed down the Telegraph Line from Dawson to Vancouver via Hazelton on September 24, 1901. Radio had not yet arrived.

In 1976, 16 drivers mushed their dog teams over the original route to commemorate those early fearless drivers. Terry McBride, a lawyer friend, and I skied along behind on the trail packed by their sleds.

In the dim pre-dawn night, we hitched a ride from Whitehorse in the truck of a musher who had partied all the previous night.

"Open that six-pack, will you?" he said soon after turning off the Alaska Highway onto the Carcross Road. "I'm dehydrated, and I need some breakfast."

Grasping a bottle in his hand, he hugged the steering wheel as the road twisted and swung through spruce forest. The white summit ridges of Mount Lorne to our left were thrown into sharp relief by the rising sun. Our driver stopped at the Caribou Hotel in

Carcross for more beer; we wondered how he would fare out on the trail.

In the hotel coffee shop resided a parrot, a replacement for the famous old bird Polly who had died recently at the age of 125 years. Described as "the oldest, meanest, ugliest, dirtiest bird north of the 60th parallel," Polly came to Carcross during the gold rush and lived thereafter in the hotel. Her owner was Captain Alexander of Engineer Mine. A temperance-minded owner of the hotel cut off Polly's liquor and tried to clean up her language by teaching her *Onward Christian Soldiers* and *I Love You Truly*. When she died, she was given a proper funeral and taken to the Carcross cemetery in a special casket. Johnny Johns, a legendary Carcross Indian elder and big game guide, gave a eulogy, and a wake was held in the Caribou Hotel.

Terry McBride and I had coffee in the hotel and then went next door to Matthew Watson's store to buy some chocolate bars for the trip. On the shore of Nares Lake, we clamped on our wooden cross-country skis and set off as the sun was coming up over the shoulder of Montana Mountain. We carried only light day packs, since the mushers were carrying our camping gear. The wind followed behind us and the temperature was a balmy minus six degrees Celsius.

As we turned into Windy Arm, a chill blast blew off the peaks at the head of the lake, and a vortex of snow spiralled skywards from convection currents that sucked up light powder on the lake surface. We slithered across sastrugi (bare icy ridges and hummocks) that scraped the wax off our skis. This left them without grip, and we slipped back with every forward stride. A fine spin drift of blown ice crystals, which snaked across the ground and swirled around our feet, made patterns that danced against the sunlight. Our morale ebbed fast on Windy Arm. The teams that passed us had an easier time; the dogs' moccasin bootees gripped well on the crisp icy surface.

In the shelter of trees at the foot of Striker's Pass, we re-waxed our skis. A gentle climb brought us to the top of the pass, where water ran in an open creek. Anticipating the long day's work ahead, we drank long and deep. The climbing sun of the spring equinox made the woods glow. Three dog teams had stopped at the same spot and, contrary to discipline, a pair was coupling in the traces. Rending the air with strong language, the mushers separated them.

At the top of the pass, the trail, spotted with the diarrhoea of excited dogs, was switch-backed with short, bumpy moguls. Four hours later, we rested on a log. The trail from the pass to the shores of Tagish Lake was a narrow, deep-cut track, allowing little room for us to brake by snowploughing. We shot down the hill out of control and crashed head first into a snow bank — our skis in the air and our mouths full of snow. The dog sleds had fared little better, judging by the flotsam left after their encounters with ill-sited trees.

The trail levelled across a neck of land where low-angled shafts of evening light filtered through bare, skeletal poplars. The silence was broken by the swish of skis and the dull crunch of poles in the snow crust beside the trail. Terry and I emerged from the woods at a small Indian cabin, where some dog teams were resting. Our legs felt leaden, and supper was still another dozen miles away down Talaha Bay. The volcanic cone of Mount Minto stood out against a glowering grey cloud to the east behind Moose Arm, where we would camp.

On arriving at the Moose Arm cabin, we gulped some stew left over in a common pot, and drank cold beer that had been sent out by well-wishers from Atlin. We pitched our bivouac tent on the lake — as far away as possible from the cabin where dog mushers were revelling and a host of noisy dogs barked. Above us was a vault of stars and a new kettle moon. Both the stillness of the starry night and our sleep were punctuated by yelping, fighting, and mating malamutes, Siberian huskies, and plain old mongrels. Raising their heads skywards, they emitted long baleful howls that were accompanied by the angry descant of mushers.

Terry McBride resting on Atlin Lake during the Carcross - Atlin mail run.

At 3:30 a.m., I built a fire in the cook tent with wood set aside the previous night. I brewed a big pot of sweet tea, which I forced on Terry, who was reluctant even to put an arm out of his warm sleeping bag to hold the mug. An hour later, we stepped into our ski bindings and set off to follow the trail in the bland morning greyness.

Ten kilometres out, we struck Jones Lake and tried to stay in the trees along the lake shore to avoid the danger of spring snow melt overflow on the ice. At the end of the lake, we were forced to follow a compass bearing through the woods because we couldn't find the sinuous trail known as Pigtail Portage. Entering thick dead fall timber, we climbed around and over giant tree trunks — an awkward manoeuver on skis. As the morning temperature rose, the snow in the forest softened and, after two exhausting hours of sinking through the crust, we skied out of some thin aspen and onto the firm surface of Atlin Lake. While we stopped for a drink and a rest, a dog sled appeared out of the trees just north of where we sat;

we had been slogging through dead fall and deep snow for two hours and the proper trail had been right beside us the entire time!

We skied 30 kilometres down the lake to Atlin. Sometimes we were in the company of dog teams; other times alone. The mountains around the lake shone under the sun's glare and seemed to stand high like Himalayan giants. Rounding the corner of Fourth of July Bay, we saw the ice alive with people taking part in Atlin Fun Days, an annual festival to celebrate the arrival of spring. Children played hockey in front of the Atlin Inn, and hot dog stalls did a brisk business. There were obstacle ski races and dog sled rides for children.

Norman Fisher, the doyen of old-time mail drivers, officially welcomed the 16 dog teams. Nearly 90 years old, he wore his Seaforth Highlanders glengarry bonnet and a fur-trimmed parka. Terry and I were introduced to him, and he talked about his arrival in Atlin and about the old days on the mail run.

"I went to Dawson in 1902 hoping to mine," he said. "Finding ten men after every job, I moved south to Atlin. After the first flush of the gold rush had subsided, Atlin had just 5,000 people and nine saloons. I tried working at a sawmill, mining on McKee Creek, and hydraulicking on Spruce Creek. Then I surveyed, dug, and did some blacksmithing on Boulder Creek. In 1904, I joined the mail service."

In the summer, the Royal Mail was carried by boat under contract between the government and the British Yukon Navigation Company. The company's mandate was

To convey, or cause to be conveyed, His Majesty's mails once per week each way during the summer season between Atlin and Caribou Crossing on and from opening of navigation to close of navigation.

The winter mail was carried by horse-drawn sleigh or dog sled. One mining engineer's wife recorded travelling on the stage to Atlin to join her husband, who was working the creeks. A team of two bay horses hauled an open sleigh, and the passengers sat on grain sacks and hay bales. The fare was fifteen dollars each and three cents a pound for baggage. Children from Atlin would go out to Third Island to wait for the stagecoach to appear and then hitch their sleds to the rear for a ride back to town.

Before the departure of the last boat of the season from Atlin at the end of October, there was often a hectic night of blackjack. Many miners lost all their summer earnings; some had to stay for the winter and trap to pay off their gambling debts. After freeze-up, the mail was carried by sled over the lake ice. Each sled carried about 200 kilograms of mail.

The Carcross–Atlin mail run was reputedly the toughest in Canada. A good trip took three days; a bad one, twelve. The first stage to Squaw Point Roadhouse followed Tagish Lake and Taku Arm. The second stage was to Moose Arm Roadhouse. There, the drivers met the Atlin mail team, and cargoes were exchanged. Another route was from Log Cabin to Tepee, Fantail Lake, Golden Gate on Tagish Lake, and then to Taku Landing.

The Canadian Pacific Railway boat that carried the mail used to dock in Skagway every ten days up to Christmas and then every two weeks until May. The mail then travelled by White Pass & Yukon Railway to Carcross (each train load carrying about 300 kilograms of mail). From Carcross, Jack McMurphy ran the mail from 1928 to 1932. His chief partners were Leo Taku Jack, Henry Taku Jack, and Paul Tingley. In good conditions, they drove two teams of six dogs each. McMurphy went through the ice on six different occasions, but his dogs always dragged him out to safety. Once, when he was soaked to the waist, his pant legs froze like stovepipes, and he had great difficulty in running behind the sled.

He also delivered mail to Engineer Mine. One Christmas, he had to deliver two separate loads: one of mail; the other, liquor. He dropped his mail cargo first, and then, on December 24, he made a very hard second journey to get the liquor to the miners in time for their Christmas party. He arrived with the second cargo to find the whole camp already drunk; someone in Carcross had mistakenly switched the two loads of freight.

Dog teams usually travelled in pairs so that mushers could help each other out of trouble. In the event that the sled went through the ice, the driver kept a small can of gasoline and a waterproof container of matches handy so that he could light a fire. In November 1902, two mail carriers, McIntyre and Abbey, disappeared on the return trip from Atlin to Log Cabin. A search party found Abbey's hat and then discovered the sled, which was floating under the ice nearby. The drowned dogs were still in their traces, and the bodies of the two drivers lay close together in shallow ice water. The searchers retrieved the mail, dried it out, and forwarded it to its proper destinations.

Norman Fisher made light of the difficulties of the mail run.

"There's nothing much to being on the mail except driving dogs and getting wet once in a while," he said. "But it's hard work. If a man watches his dogs, he can learn how to be comfortable. I learned more from my dogs than they ever learned from me. Most of the hard trips on the mail were just caused by goddamned foolishness."

Norman once took fourteen days from Atlin to Log Cabin. On that trip, he was accompanied by Captain Alexander.

"We got into all kinds of jackpots," he said. "The lake was open at Golden Gate, so we had to spend four or five days building a raft. We used an axe and some light rope. Then we started across open water, battling a wind that blew the ice towards us. Our six dogs struggled all night to stay on the raft while I steered a course around the ice. Finally, we reached an island and sheltered from the storm. But the ice moved in and marooned us with very little grub for ourselves or the dogs."

Norman took a breath and continued in his matter-of-fact way.

"A strip of water opened up towards evening on the third day. We placed the mail and two exhausted dogs on the raft, expecting the others to swim. However, all but one of the dogs climbed on the raft, sinking it. From then on, we waded sloughs and crossed rivers, reaching Tepee late at night on May 31, twelve days after setting off from Atlin. All of the next day, we tramped through tussock grass, reaching the Tutshi River near Log Cabin by evening."

Norman refused to leave the mail and the dogs, so Alexander swam across the river and walked two hours to Log Cabin for help. He and another mail driver built a raft to cross the river to where Norman was waiting.

"We loaded the mail and the dogs onto the raft and began the return trip," he said. "When we were nearly across, the current began to drive us into a set of rapids. Alexander saved the day by jumping ashore and tethering the raft to a tree with a rope. On another occasion, my dogs were getting tired, so I decided to unharness them early in the day. As soon as I removed the traces, a couple of caribou appeared and the dogs took off. One dog returned without its pack of mail. I searched the thick muskeg for the mail, but no luck. Another time, near Tagish Ferry, my sleigh dropped through the rotten spring ice. It got hung up on a small pinnacle of rock in about two metres of water. I couldn't raise the loaded sleigh alone, so I plunged into the water to lift it off one bag at a time. That mail was damn well moist, I tell you."

Norman relit his pipe, took a couple of long puffs and, with such an attentive audience, he launched himself again into another of his stories.

"One of my hardest trips came one fall when the weather turned cold early. I was paddling across Tagish Lake in a canoe at minus 50 degrees Celsius against a strong north wind. Finally the fellow with me, who was leaning over the bow breaking the ice, said, 'I can't do any more. I'm done in.' Then he passed out. After a while he came to again and we struggled to shore. That was mighty hard. I thought we'd had it, but we made out alright once we lit a fire."

Norman Fisher went to France in 1916 with the 72nd Seaforth Highlanders. On his last night in France, Norman's platoon was cut to pieces in the trenches by shellfire and only two men survived. Norman stopped in a big shell hole to get directions and looked up to see a small long-range shell coming straight for him — "Just like a baseball." He dived headfirst into another deep hole and the flying shell went off just where his feet had been seconds before. Later that night, shrapnel took the tops off three of his fingers.

When Norman returned from the war, he spent a few years prospecting all over northern British Columbia. He bought a pleasure boat, the *Prowler*, for taking tourists on trips and also for booming logs across to the sawmill. When he retired, he was still a bachelor.

"I was thinking about getting married before the war came along," he said. "But then I thought I'd like to see one war anyway. I'm too cranky for one woman to get along with, so now I get along with all of them. I smoke my pipe, split enough wood for the day, and play chess at night. Lots of times in my life I moved in the right direction at the right time, which is mostly luck. If there's a next life, I suppose I'll probably be just as lucky as I was here, and if there isn't, I'll be lucky anyway."

Terry McBride and I reluctantly dragged ourselves away from Norman Fisher's stories of those noble old days. We went to Wayne Merry's sauna, built in a corner of his back barn, to soothe our aching muscles and steam ourselves until our skin was wrinkled like prunes.

By nightfall, a party was in full swing in the Moose Hall, which stands on First Street between Arthur Mitchell's hardware store and the RCMP detachment. Built in Discovery in 1905, it was the home of Camp 19 of the Arctic Brotherhood. In the 1920s, the building was moved to Atlin by John Noland. He cut it into three sections and, using a team of horses, dragged them, one at a time, on log skids. The reconstructed building originally stood next to the Nugget Saloon. During dances, people could slip into the saloon through a side exit.

This night, the floor heaved up and down with the gyrations of the dancers. We gambled our money away to a croupier, who tucked dollar bills down her bosom or into her garter. The heat of the room melted snow under the floorboards so, when anyone stomped on the floor, water seeped up into a big puddle. Someone drilled a couple of holes in the floor for drainage, but this worked in reverse. With each prance a jet of water spouted out of the floor and shot up the dancers' legs.

"Looks like clam-diggin' time back east," said one lady, who went home to fetch her gum boots.

Terry McBride and I left the Moose Hall while the party was still in full swing. Having fully relived the Carcross-Atlin mail run, we collapsed exhausted into our beds.

Christmas in Atlin

For the first few years after we acquired the cabin, our winter visits to Atlin became less frequent. When snow arrived in Whitehorse at the beginning of October, the family became busy with cross-country skiing. Most days of the week, both Adam and Judith trained after school with their coach, Father Jean Mouchet. They used skinny fibreglass skis to race on the ski club's groomed trails and turned up their noses at thrashing across country through the bush with their father. Adam went for a month to ski at Father Mouchet's home village in France to be exposed to the European ski culture. Judith was the youngest member of a victorious Yukon relay team at the Canadian National Junior championships, which were held in Whitehorse.

Meanwhile, Lucy refused to put on skis at all until Sarah bribed her with some Muppets to descend the very gentle incline behind our house. A mysterious conversion followed, and twelve years later she was competing for Canada at the 1992 Winter Olympic Games. Sarah kept the home on an even keel and occasionally went down-hill skiing, a sport at which she had excelled as a teenager. I skied fanatically in Whitehorse with two other old fogey athletes; we made up in enthusiasm what we lacked in technique.

One cold day in early December, Adam and I set off towards Atlin to prepare the cabin for Christmas. On the way, we planned to visit Hector MacKenzie, a friend who lived in Tagish. Light snow crystals and then big flakes floated out of a leaden sky, where heavy clouds threatened more snowfall.. We drove our old station wagon down the Alaska Highway and turned off at Jake's Corner.

Halfway along the Tagish Road, we saw a moose standing in the middle of the road. We coasted slowly towards him as he gazed at our approaching headlights with scorn. When the car was only a few metres away, he nodded his full rack of antlers and haughtily ambled off into a grove of aspen beside the road. The muscles of his huge haunches were taut and ridged as he floundered through the soft snow, which came almost up to his underbelly.

"Watch out, Dad!" exclaimed Adam. At the same time, I heard a dull crunch as the car slid gently off the road and into a hidden snow-filled ditch. I tried to jack up the back of the car and tip it sideways, but a few minutes of work showed this approach to be useless. The highway was deserted.

"Let's ski to the Old Trading Post and ask Hector to pull us out," I said.

We clamped on our skis and swished along the road on a skiff of new snow. Snowflakes settling on the trees added magic to the peace of the morning. We covered the ten kilometres to Tagish in less than an hour and reached the Old Trading Post where lived the MacKenzie family, who are as Scottish as their name. On hearing of our predicament, Hector immediately drove us back to our stranded car.

We dug snow away with shovels and put willow brush under the wheels for grip. Hector then fixed a doubled climbing rope to our back axle and pulled us out. We were soon motoring back to the Trading Post, a log house set on a creek that flows into a bay off Tagish Lake. When I first came to the Yukon ahead of the family, I spent several summer weekends there paddling a canoe up the creek beside their house and watching the many wading birds that congregate in the bay.

"Come in and warm up," said Ann MacKenzie. "How about some tea and scones?"

Our paths had crossed several times before over the years. Ann had arrived to work as an assistant cook at the Eskdale Outward Bound School in the English Lake District as I was leaving after a stint as a temporary instructor. Five years later, she became the housekeeper at the hospital in North West River, Labrador, where Sarah and I were working. Ten years later, when I came to prospect a job in the Yukon, Ann and I bumped into each other on Main Street in Whitehorse. Then, for the first time, I met her husband, a wilderness guide and avalanche expert.

"You'd better stay for the night," Hector said. Adam and I readily acquiesced, since it was getting late. We settled in front of the wood stove and listened to stories of the MacKenzies' homesteading life. We decided to postpone our attempt to reach Atlin until the next weekend. That time we were successful.

A year later, Judith and I set off down the Alaska Highway on another similar pre-Christmas expedition. In the mid-winter darkness, curtains of blue, green, purple, and pink Northern Lights swarmed across the sky. I was wary of the beauty however, because the Northern Lights often warn of an advancing cold front. The thermometer registered minus 40 degrees Celsius, and it hurt to breathe. While loosening the gas cap, I made the cheechako's (or greenhorn's) mistake of holding the car keys momentarily in my mouth. My moist lips froze to the metal and some skin was painfully removed in the process of thawing the key free. We refuelled and, because of the very cold weather, added some wood alcohol to absorb any water that had condensed in the gas tank and might block the fuel line.

We ate a chocolate bar from our emergency food pack and drove into the night. A red light appeared on the dashboard beside the water temperature gauge. I halted on the roadside, taking care not to park too close to the shoulder. A grader-operator had scraped snow with his blade well out over the ditch, so it looked as if firm ground extended farther out than it truly did. On opening the hood, I could see by the flashlight that steam was leaking from a crack in the radiator hosing and was pouring into the frosty air. Water trickled onto the hot engine and evaporated instantly. I had tools in the trunk, but there was no spare hosing or anything with which to repair the crack.

Judith put on her ski overpants and jacket to keep out the biting cold. The road was deserted of traffic, so we lit a fire both to draw attention to ourselves and to keep warm. We tried to reach some dead fall trees close to the road to get some firewood, but without snowshoes we stumbled thigh deep in soft snow. Skis would have been useless in the bottomless snow and the tightly woven ground willow. Eventually, I got some deadwood, which we broke and sawed up. The exercise warmed us and boosted our morale, but as soon as the fire caught ice crystals melted and dampened the flame. Soon, lights approached from the north and a sports car drew up.

"Hi, need a hand?" drawled an American voice. The driver gave us some sticky aluminum duct tape to patch the cracked hosing.

"Many thanks for stopping," I said. "Where are you going?"

"California." he said. "Only 4,000 miles to the sun. Be seein' ya." He drove on into the dim light of the aurora.

After taping the crack, we needed to refill the drained radiator. We tried thawing snow on the fire, but it took ages and we needed a quart or more; so we peed into a saucepan. Taking a chance on driving with a half-full radiator, I started the car. The red light stayed off, so I gingerly drove onward. Soon, however, the sinister "hot" light flickered on again, the air heater blew cold, and the car stopped. The circulating hot water had melted the tape, and water had poured onto the engine again. An overpowering stench of ammonia drove us from under the hood, and we got back into the car.

In the trunk, we carried full cold weather survival gear and a tent, but we chose not to pitch it in case a ride came along. The car cooled rapidly, so Judith curled up in a corner in my old Everest sleeping bag while I sat wearing all my down clothing.

Half an hour later, a jeep drew up and, the driver, who was a trucker going from Texas to Alaska to collect a vehicle, offered us a ride. He put out a call to other drivers on his citizen-band two-way radio.

"I ask them about weather conditions and police speed traps," he said. "It breaks the monotony of pounding icy roads for long hours."

He drove us back along the highway and dropped us off at a friend's house. It was nearly midnight.

"Walked from Whitehorse?" my friend asked laconically. "We'd better go and fetch the car. You can't leave it on the highway for the night without lights. Let's tuck Judith into bed."

With various tools and bits of rubber piping, we set off in his truck back to my stranded car. Water from the radiator had iced up the engine and the wiring, so we lit a Coleman stove and shoved it underneath the oil pan. For half an hour, we struggled with rock-hard rubber piping. Eventually, after nearly freezing our fingers tightening the small nuts and bolts of the hose clamps, we were able to replace the fractured section. We wore the battery down from trying to turn the starter motor and used the truck battery to boost it, but we had to give up trying to fix the radiator because the water in the circulating heater lines had frozen.

We hooked a tow-rope to the truck's rear bracket and set off for Jake's Corner. I steered with my head out of the window because the windscreen was opaque with ice crystals. The freezing metal of the car body creaked and the tires, frozen out of shape, lurched drunkenly.

Travelling at 50 kilometres per hour in a temperature of minus 40 degrees Celsius created a wind-chill equivalent to more than 70 degrees below zero. My eyelashes were frosted so badly that I could hardly see, and, despite wearing two balaclavas, my nose and cheeks felt numb and hard. My hands were so cold I could barely steer. The horn groaned like a tired bullfrog when I tried to warn my friend to slow down. I fixed my eyes on his truck's tail-lights and hoped for the best.

A double semi-trailer truck approached and threw up a cloud of snow from the heavy tread of its studded winter tires. Blinded by the spin drift, I slid into a snowbank. My friend's truck was jerked to a halt and its wheels spun on the icy road. The driver of a following south-bound truck pulled me out backwards onto the road. In less than five minutes, he was trundling towards balmier climes. At 3 a.m., we reached Jake's Corner. I was semi-frozen, exhausted, and totally fed up.

The next morning, Jake did a patch-up job that enabled us to drive back to Whitehorse. Exasperated with our station wagon's never-ending complaints, we sold the behemoth for a song and bought a small Japanese car that was much better suited for winter driving in the North.

As Christmas drew near, we made plans for going to the cabin. Feeling intimately the spell that has entrapped us in this deserted, inclement land, Sarah, Lucy, and I drove through the silent wilderness. Adam and Judith preferred to hang out with their friends in Whitehorse until the last possible moment; they would follow later.

Lucy was in mourning for Hazel, the dear five-year-old rabbit that she had acquired one halcyon summer while staying at the Pelly River Ranch. Three days before Christmas, she had gone downstairs to feed him in the utility room, where he was confined to keep him from molesting our grand motherly, twenty-five pound cat Maude. Hazel roamed free under the workbench and around the back of the clothes dryer.

Lucy found him peacefully and terminally asleep on the mat under a chair. With his passing, she lost her closest confidant in times of stress, sadness, anger, or parental variance. Our family grief was poignant. I dug a grave for Mr. Rabbit in the frozen ground among the willow bushes beyond our back fence. We held a proper funeral and left immediately afterwards for Atlin.

The thin layer of snow that covered the ice on Marsh Lake stood out against the sombre cohorts of dark green lodge pole pine and spruce. In the thin morning light, the hoarfrost-rimed willow and aspen branches looked like delicate wire sculptures. Ice crystals, suspended in the air, sparkled in the low sun that was making its brief winter solstice appearance over the mountain tops.

The cold weather had firmly cemented snow to the gravel surface of the Atlin Road. A lynx, his hairy feet making large footprints in the snow, darted out from the ditch, ran down the road ahead of us, and then dived into the bush. There, his tufted ears pricked up on alert, he stood still and watched us.

Atlin Mountain looked massive compared with its snowless summer form. A cloud of steam hung above scattered areas of open water at the unfrozen north end of Atlin Lake and at the mouth of Torres Channel. One night before Christmas, the ice suddenly shifted in a south wind and left open water in front of town out beyond Third Island. The lake churned as dense cold water sank to the bottom and warmer water surfaced. Steam clung like icing sugar to the trees on First Island.

Sleepiness pervaded Atlin town, and few people stirred. The cabin was like an icebox when we arrived. A bottle of pop inadvertently left in the fridge had exploded and had blown the door wide open. The remains of the bottle had been showered throughout the cabin. Sarah lit the wood-burning stove in the kitchen and stoked it to raise the oven temperature high enough for cooking. I fired up the double-skinned barrel furnace in the basement, fed it metre-long logs, and opened the door vent until the furnace roared like an old steam train. After a couple of hours, heat percolated through the little house and seeped into the walls. Frost coated the front door sill, where cold outside air and the hot inside air mingled.

We crossed the road to visit the Merrys for a couple of hours. On our return, the cabin was warm and snug, but the water in our kitchen barrel had frozen to a block of ice that took another two days to thaw out. Meanwhile, we filled buckets with lake water which we collected through a hole cut in the ice in front of town.

Choosing a Christmas tree was a serious family ritual, because the tree had to be a suitable size and shape and also had to be of the correct species. Spruce have brittle dead lower branches that readily shed needles. The upward curving fronds of balsam exude sweet pine resin, but they only grow in small stands near the Warm Springs. Some people in the north use artificial Christmas trees so that they have no fallen needles to clean up on Twelfth Night. Once, when visiting an Inuit chief in Labrador, I was surprised to find him opening a mail order parcel containing a fold-down plastic Christmas tree. But, for us, artificial trees don't hold the same spell as a real tree.

We drove out along the Warm Bay Road to select a tree from among the millions that cover our wilderness. Carrying an axe and a saw, we tramped through the snow in our mukluks. Large tracks, signs of moose high-stepping into their silent world beyond our view, led off into the bush. Lucy espied a shapely tree: a fir with elegant branches held out like the arms of a pirouetting dancer. We felled it carefully so the frozen branches wouldn't snap off.

Lucy placed the tree in front of the cabin window that faced the lake and First Island, which looked bare without my sailboat moored there. She decorated it with coloured lights and the hand-crafted hangings that Sarah had collected from all over the world. We hung Christmas cards on a ribbon and piled presents under the tree.

The cabin in winter.

On Christmas Eve, Judith and Adam arrived, having caught a ride with a friend. After a family supper, we walked around the town. New-fallen snow blanketed the log buildings and evoked images of times long past. Smoke rose vertically in the still air from a hundred chimneys, and we smelled the fragrance of burning pine and aspen.

The bell in the tower of the Catholic Church beside the Indian village tolled a summons to midnight mass. Our breath steaming, we padded through the crunchy snow. Snowflakes glinted in the light from the street lamps, and figures drifted out of the dark towards the church. The light from the open door was a beacon that beckoned in the night. A blast of hot air hit us as we entered; Father Plaine was stoking the barrel stove in the middle of the nave. Wearing his off-white cassock belted with a rope ceinture, he busied himself with preparing the sacraments in the curtained sanctuary alcove.

Most of the Taku Tlingit adults gathered in the back rows, while their children kneeled near the front. Scattered among them were other Catholic parishioners. Father Plaine emerged from the vestry. His tonsure was surrounded by grey hair, and his high-bossed forehead invited polishing. He stared through thick spectacles, and his brow, furrowed like a newly ploughed field, gave him a look of constant surprise. His sudden smiles would screw up his eyes so that crowsfeet radiated from the horizon of his cheekbones. His skin was wrinkled from exposure to wind and cold during the many tough journeys he had made by dog sled across the northern Yukon in his younger days. Protruding ears suggested that he might take off in flight in a stiff breeze. He spoke with vivid gestures of his hands, and his Adam's apple bobbed up and down as his throaty voice extolled the spiritual life to his flock.

We sang carols with vigour. After the blessing, we left and kicked our way through new-fallen snow as we would with dead leaves in autumn. Chill water lapped the shore and formed ice on the pebbles and boulders. Sarah and I stayed up late, filled the children's stockings with small gifts, and then climbed into our queen-sized bunk bed along with our fat, warm cat Maude. Lucy was on the bunk above us, while Adam and Judith slept out in the porch, which had been insulated the previous summer against the impending winter. But Jack Frost still formed crazy opaque patterns on the window panes, and a draft under the front door made a ruff of frost against the sill. The house cooled as the crackling of logs ceased and the furnace died.

On Christmas morning, snow hung heavy in the clouds. I planned to ski to Noland Mine with the children, but Lucy, who preferred to stay home and help Sarah prepare Christmas dinner, declined. Adam, Judith, and I drove up to Spruce Creek, where we put on skis and left the road to make our own tracks. The trail to Noland Mine climbed steadily to an open space, where a shortcut to Discovery by way of Stevendyke Creek began. The trail divided:

to the left was the trail up Blue Canyon (so named because of the forget-me-nots in spring and blueberries and moss berries in summer); to the right the trail led to Noland Mine.

We skied over rolling terrain dotted with pine and balsam. From the open ground, we could see distant rounded hills. Snowflakes crusted our eyelashes and caked our eyebrows. Suddenly we were overlooking the edge of the creek rim. Barely visible in the snowstorm was a ghostly village of abandoned mine buildings and the deserted site of some gold diggings. These were nestled into a fold of the hillside at the head of a small valley into which the canyon debouched. Snow formed jagged patterns on the buckets of a huge wheel that was originally from the steamboat *Scotia* and had been converted into a water-wheel. The tall mine shaft tower and mill wheel stood out above some weathered log cabin bunkhouses, the mess hall, and engine shop.

We skied down the hill and passed a two-storey house with an elegant balcony where the mine manager had once lived. Beside it was a roofless shed. Snow had sunk between the skeleton of its rafters and had formed swags that hung down like skeins of wool. Pieces of machinery lay about as though someone had torn the mine apart in anger, scattering the pieces far and wide.

We have returned to this site several times since, but never has Noland Mine appeared so eerie as on that first visit. Its emptiness was a stark contrast to a century before, when Spruce Creek was busy with miners who had lived in shacks along its length. In underground shafts and surface placer operations, they scraped enough gold flakes off the bedrock to make a meagre living.

On our return to Atlin, we skied down to the dock where *Ven* was moored. I had left her in the water unusually, and foolishly, late. We chipped a ruff of ice off the hull at water level, swept snow from the deck, loosened the frozen mainsheet with wood alcohol, and set sail. A brisk breeze blew us around Third Island, chased the ice fog away, and stirred up the lake surface. We celebrated being the silliest sailors north of 60 degrees latitude that Christmas Day by

opening a box of rum-flavored chocolates. Then we headed for our
mooring and hauled the boat out onto her trailer before the slip-
way became too icy to allow traction.

We returned to a cosy, warm cabin and to a feast prepared by
Sarah and Lucy — this despite the uneven heat of the wood stove
and its oven that was difficult to get hot enough without roasting
everyone in the house. Occasionally, Sarah opened the front door
to cool the room and a cloud of vapour blew in as the crisp air
condensed. We had Christmas crackers to pull open, party hats to
wear, turkey and plum pudding to eat, and games of shove-half
penny to play. Then we all went off to sing carols in the Anglican
church in descant with the booming voices of Tom Kirkwood and
Krist Johnsen and in counterpoint with Win Acheson and Vera
Kirkwood. I am no chorister (having been turned down for a place
in the choir at North West River, Labrador by my two closest
friends: the minister and the choirmaster), but Krist was even more
out of tune than me.

On Boxing Day the temperature fell to 40 degrees below zero.
By midday, Adam and I felt restive. Bright sun beckoned, but it was
too cold to ski, so we dressed warmly, put moose hide mukluks on
our feet, and went for a walk in the woods behind the Indian village. A snowy blanket filled the hollows and ironed out the rough-
ness of the land. We followed a well-packed trail of snowshoe tracks
that led towards Graham's Farm and the Indian Cemetery. The previous summer, we had seen a huge hawk gliding lazily and an owl
perched in the trees, but they were no longer there. All was still and
silent. A pure white arctic snowshoe hare with ruffs around its ankles scampered into the bush and left wide tracks in the snow. Its
home was under one of the big pines, and it fed on willow bark
in the marsh.

Deep snow on the esker of the valley slowed us. A coyote had
left tracks, and, nearby, some bigger paw marks went off in a straight
line; wolves were coming unusually close to town that winter. After an hour, we dropped down a bank to Graham's Farm. There,

we lit a fire under a big spruce tree using twigs snapped from close to the trunk for tinder. The bright flames gave off little heat, but the fire gave us an excuse to stop and rest for a while.

We headed home. On the alkali flats we found recent moose prints and some snowshoe tracks — the common rat-tail pattern, not the elegant Teslin snowshoe that curves up at the toe. We nearly tripped over a spruce partridge that was trying to burrow into an earthy overhanging bank. The sun set behind Atlin Mountain, the streetlights shone in the gathering dusk, and a thin pall of ice-fog rolling off the freezing lake hung in the twilight.

Back in the cabin, Sarah made hot-buttered rum. We stoked the furnace and settled down to relish our Christmas books and to finish off a jigsaw puzzle. In the darkness outside, we could have hung our kettle on yet another sickle moon.

Epilogue

It is now twenty years since our family arrived in the North; we've lived here longer than any other place. Much has changed; and much has stayed the same — our Atlin cabin in particular. The children are all leading their own lives. Adam works in computer mathematics in Montreal; Judith lives next door to us in Whitehorse with our grandson Tim; and Lucy, who is still on the Canadian cross-country ski team, was married this year on the *Tarahne*. Sarah, as marriage commissioner, officiated. Having sold *Ven*, I am now the proud owner of the *Arctic Tern*.

A handful of years ago, Sarah and I tried to emigrate south to lotus-land. She loved it, but I lasted only six months. On a blustery, wet Victoria day, I thought the tulips were shaking their heads and mocking me, and I couldn't stand the daffodils. So we returned to our northland. Occasionally we make forays outside and relish them, but each time we come scurrying home.

Our cabin in Atlin has been the focal point to which each member of the family returns for different reasons — the space, the quiet, the wilderness, the peace. In recent years, Sarah and I have been abroad on long journeys together, but whenever the going got tough, it was to Atlin that our wandering thoughts returned.

Index

63-66, 72-73, 75, 78-80, 90-97, 103,
106, 113, 116, 134-136, 147, 153, 156,
158-163, 165, 172, 181-182, 186-187,
192-193, 198, 202, 204, 207-209, 222-
223
Mining Corporation of Canada 162
Minto *see* Mount Minto
Mitchell, Arthur 211
Mitchell, Elizabeth 181-182
Mohawks 98
Molybdenum mine 66
Monarch Mountain 87
Montana 142, 160
Montana Mountain 43, 204
Montreal 227
"Moonshine Maggie" 36
Moose 21, 46, 69, 83, 101, 104-105, 123,
133, 138, 149, 151, 159, 172, 214,
220, 224-225
Moose Arm 43, 65, 205, 208
Moose Hall 71, 211-212
Moravian missions 104
Morris, Maureen 45-46
Morton, Bruce 61
Mortuary 60-61
Mouchet, Father Jean 213
Mount Barnham mine 66
Mount Everest 20, 217
Mount Fairweather 139
Mount Lawson 41
Mount Logan 86
Mount Lorne 15, 203
Mount Minto 15, 84-85, 116, 205
Mount O'Keefe 171
Mountain climbing 20, 130-133, 138-140
Mountain goats 83, 105
Mountain sheep 85, 143, 148, 158
Mountains *see* Atlin; Bee; Birch;
Cathedral; Coastal; Florence;
Glaciers; Gleaner; Himilayas;
Llangorse; Monarch; Montana;
Mount Barnham *to* Mount
O'Keefe; Richardson; Rocky;
Section; St. Elias; Table; Tepee;
White Moose
Mounties *see* Royal Canadian Mounted
Police
Muddy Lake 198
Munich 142

Museums *see* Atlin Historical Society;
Atlin Museum

Nahlin, Joe Hicks 36
Nakina River 102, 171; country 121
Nanaimo 147
Nares 43
Nares Lake 204
Narvik 78
Nasutlin (boat) 153
Natives *see* Indians, Inuit
Nelson, Bob 58
Nelson Lake 164
Nepal 20
Never Miss Bench 135
Neville, Major Christopher William
Andrew 28-29, 107, 182, 184
New York 143, 163
New Zealand 113
Newfoundland 115
Newspapers 66, 70, 155
Noble, Captain 162
Noland, John 58, 211
Noland Mine 21, 78, 222-223
Nome 40, 63, 144, 150
Nora (boat) 165
Normandy 34
Norris Glacier 101
North Canol Road 150
North West Mounted Police 29, 40, 135
North West River (Laborador) 215, 224
Northern Airways 189-191
Northern Hotel 59
Northern lights 88, 215-216
Northern Lights College 54
Northwest Territories 150
Norway 78, 80
Nova Scotia 45, 71
Nugget Saloon 212
Nyman, Elizabeth 100

O'Connor, Dennis 56
O'Donnell River 61, 102
O'Keefe *see* Mount O'Keefe
Oblates *see* Catholics
Oka (Quebec) 98
Okalla Prison 143
Old Crow 186-187
Old Trading Post *see* Trading Post